T0012854

# The

# MODERN
# WITCHCRAFT
# Guide to
# Runes

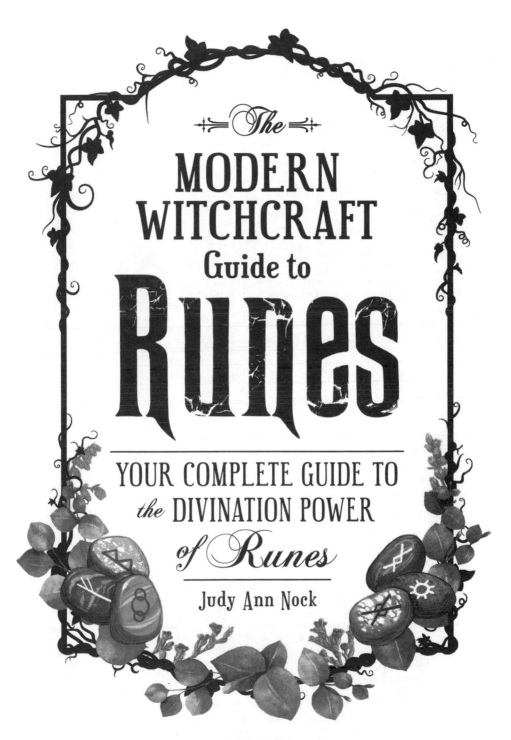

*The*

# MODERN WITCHCRAFT

## Guide to

# Runes

## YOUR COMPLETE GUIDE TO
## *the* DIVINATION POWER
## *of* Runes

Judy Ann Nock

Adams Media
New York London Toronto Sydney New Delhi

Adams Media
An Imprint of Simon & Schuster, Inc.
100 Technology Center Drive
Stoughton, Massachusetts 02072

Copyright © 2022 by
Simon & Schuster, Inc.

All rights reserved, including
the right to reproduce this book
or portions thereof in any form
whatsoever. For information address
Adams Media Subsidiary Rights
Department, 1230 Avenue of the
Americas, New York, NY 10020.

First Adams Media hardcover
edition February 2022

ADAMS MEDIA and colophon are
trademarks of Simon & Schuster.

For information about special
discounts for bulk purchases,
please contact Simon & Schuster
Special Sales at 1-866-506-1949 or
business@simonandschuster.com.

The Simon & Schuster Speakers
Bureau can bring authors to your
live event. For more information or
to book an event contact the
Simon & Schuster Speakers Bureau
at 1-866-248-3049 or visit our
website at www.simonspeakers.com.

Interior design by Priscilla Yuen
Interior illustrations by Katrina
Machado and Priscilla Yuen
Interior images © 123RF/Elena
Medvedeva; Getty Images/
bauhaus1000

Manufactured in the United States of
America

2 2022

Library of Congress Cataloging-in-
Publication Data
Names: Nock, Judy Ann, author.
Title: The modern witchcraft guide
to runes / Judy Ann Nock.
Description: Stoughton,
Massachusetts: Adams Media,
2022. | Series: Modern witchcraft |
Includes bibliographical references
and index.
Identifiers: LCCN 2021043840 |
ISBN 9781507217566 (hc) |
ISBN 9781507217573 (ebook)
Subjects: LCSH: Witchcraft. |
Runes. | Magic.
Classification: LCC BF1566 .N63
2022 | DDC 133.4/3--dc23/
eng/20211007
LC record available at
https://lccn.loc.gov/2021043840

ISBN 978-1-5072-1756-6
ISBN 978-1-5072-1757-3 (ebook)

Many of the designations used
by manufacturers and sellers to
distinguish their products are
claimed as trademarks. Where those
designations appear in this book and
Simon & Schuster, Inc., was aware of
a trademark claim, the designations
have been printed with initial capital
letters.

*To my daughter, Jaime,*
*who has been there with me, beside me,*
*every step of the way*

# *Acknowledgments*

Without the support of the following people, this book would not have been possible. To my agent, June Clark; my editor, Eileen Mullan; my daughter, Jaime Olsen, for her substantial contributions, including numerous digital drawings based on my original sketches; Peter Archer, for his skillful edits and endless patience; my inspiring friends Ann Gaba, Stephanie Duty, Llisa Jones, Tracy Peterson, Debby Schwartz, Samantha Franklin, Dena Moes, Greg Ayres, Gretchen Greaser, Leigh Brown, Julie Gillis, Barbara McGlamery, Shaula Chambliss, Jeffrey McGriff, Louie Zhelesnik, Andrew Gilchrist, Kris Sayler, Karyn Kuhl, Christian Day, Donna Distefano, Melissa Whitehead, Jamie Roach, and Tara Mathieu; and my supportive family, James and Bonnie Nock, Robert Nock, Teri Nock DelGaudio, Jackson Nock, Andrew DelGaudio, Jessie Nock Paniagua, Cindy and John Nock, Ben and Samantha Nock, Mary Nock, and Darra Zankman. I would like to acknowledge and thank Strand Bookstore in New York City for their support, as well as Book Culture in New York and Open Books in Pensacola, Florida, for hosting me for author events. I would like to call upon the eternal memory of my friends in spirit who were with me in the beginning, passed beyond the veil, and yet are with me still: Susan Sherrill, Will Ryan, Cayne Miceli, Tara Mooney, and Kevin Marchetti. Particularly for Susan, Cayne, and Kevin, I will always pick up a hammer and beat it against an anvil to ring out your names. To the memory of my husband of twenty-three years, David Olsen, my Viking, this book is perhaps one you may have liked, had you lived. May you be welcomed into the halls of your ancestors. May your names be spoken and your stories be told, for I am forever blessed by you. Thank you.

# CONTENTS

# ❖ PART II ❖
# CONSULTING AND ATTUNING WITH THE RUNES 103

*The Modern Witchcraft Guide to Runes*

*The Modern Witchcraft Guide to Runes*

# *Introduction*

### *Runes are a gateway to magick.*

They offer spells of protection and health. They are a guide to the future and the past. They are a gateway to a world of powers and mysteries that are almost beyond understanding. The art of runes is your passport to the never-ending realms of the spirits, places of wonder and enchantment.

From their first use around C.E. 150, runes—alphabetic figures used for communication systems in many Scandinavian countries—have been used for many different purposes. For some, runes were merely an ancient system of writing, and modern scholars have studied them that way. However, even more evidence suggests that runes were used for divination. There is even conjecture that the runes themselves are inhabited by beings who can open links to other realms.

In *The Modern Witchcraft Guide to Runes*, you'll see how casting runes gives modern witches the ability to access information previously unknown and unseen. Whether you're an experienced practicing witch or someone just beginning to explore the world of witchcraft by using this book, you'll come to understand the magick and mystery of runes.

You'll learn about the history of runes, how they were used for magickal purposes in ancient times, and how they connect to witchcraft and to the natural world that surrounds us today. You'll learn how to choose the right runic system for you, one that will strengthen your powers as a witch, and how to incorporate your chosen system (or systems) into your everyday magickal practices. And you'll discover how best to create your own runes using sustainable raw materials and engraving methods, such as carving, burning, and painting.

Your runes allow you to discern pathways and gain insight. You can use them for divination and as an oracle. For many witches, runes symbolize a connection to spirit, where messages can be transmitted from beyond the veil—from a time out of time—and interpreted in the here and now.

Finally, runes can be very personal, reminding you of the journeys—physical and spiritual—that you've taken. As you handle your runes, you'll feel a sudden spark of recognition, a memory of your own sacred origin. You'll know you are surrounded by all the magick the earth offers her inhabitants.

For modern witchcraft, runes endure as a powerful system for empowerment, fortune-telling, and gaining insight. They give you confidence and power as a witch: Your voice is worthy. Your experiences are valid. Your ideas are powerful. You are part of a community of witches and are free to define yourself in your own terms and, by using runes, bring magick and joy to your work and to the world. Blessed be your runes.

## *Chapter 1*

# RUNE BASICS: PURPOSE AND POWER

When you explore runes, you can hear the words and voices of the ancients through time. A spoken or written word has a power that allows you to tap into a timeless vibration. These runes—these symbols, and the sounds they represent—contain unbound vibrational energy rooted in, but not limited to, the past. Runes carry with them the wisdom of the ages.

## OUR TRUE PATH WILL BE DETERMINED BY OUR NATURE

Runes are inextricably linked to trees. From the Ogham tree alphabet of Ireland and Yggdrasil, the tree of life from which the Norse God Odin first spied the runes, to the painful memories of witches who were hanged from gallows trees, the way of the runes brings you back to the trees, to the beauty of the wild forest, the wonder of discovered lands, and the voices that echo across unending generations to inform the way of the modern witch. Trees are some of the longest-lived organisms on earth, and their presence and power throughout recorded history are an unbroken testament to their importance.

# THE CHALLENGE OF MAGICK

Magick such as that contained in runes is and has always been a practice fraught with difficulty. Witches have historically found themselves misunderstood, wrongly accused of misdeeds, reviled, and feared. Yet there is another side to this. Today more and more people, female, male, and nonbinary, identify as witches. The power of the witch is not only returning and revealing itself in a new and modern form; it is also rapidly growing. As more and more people discover or rediscover their propensity for magick, their rejection of societal norms, and their awareness of the danger of stereotypes, a new paradigm of the modern witch continues to evolve.

Runes are a central part of magick, the gateway to a timeless oracle, consulted freely by the practitioner with a deep hunger for knowledge. The needs of humanity today echo those of the distant past; it is into this deep well that we reach in order to draw up the knowledge carved in rock, wood, or the skeletal remains of the horned and hoofed creatures.

Approach the runes with an open mind and a guileless heart. Accept their teachings, for in their mystery is nothing less than the wisdom of the ages, distilled through generations across many lands.

Runes allow you to approach an oracle, a surrounding energy that binds you to your fate. You are the creator of your destiny, and the oracle is the aura of the culmination of your choices. It is a field of knowledge that exists out of time itself. When you consult the oracle through runes, you bring inquiries, needs, dreams, and desires. Your heart is filled with longing. Every hope that lies inside you is laid bare. When you openly seek, you must admit your own limitations, including vulnerability and fallibility.

Pick up a tool. Feel its weight in your hands. Be willing to strike, to change, to fail. Swing a hammer, driving steel into metal, and listen for the song of the blow: You will hear some tones that have a high pitch and some that have a low pitch. This vibration has been echoing across the earth since the Bronze Age when the first writing systems began to appear.

By the first century, the Elder Futhark writing script was in use. This is where our journey begins, in the distant past of northern Europe when people recorded their needs and their requests to the Gods in metal and stone. This is what constitutes the oracle.

Like a surrounding whisper that was never silenced, the oracle has endured from the beginning of time. The runes are an entry point, the gateway to an esoteric language of mystery that has spanned continents, eras, and civilizations. Yet the farther you get from the source, the closer you actually become, because the energy moves in a great cosmic spiral that is constantly turning in on itself even as it is expanding.

## The Energy of Runes

The radiating, unseen energy of runes is similar to heat; you can't see it, but you can't deny it, and it has transformative powers over elements such as iron. That is the reason why runes became known during the Iron Age. Their energy had always been contained deep in the earth, where there is intense power. Once runes were discovered, everything changed.

Imagine the power of the written word, the power to communicate and have messages endure. This in itself is a powerful form of magick. The growing ability of human beings to manipulate their environment through the use of tools brought them to the crossroads where creative, transformative energy met spirit. Through the act of transformation, changing natural materials from one thing into another, vibrational energy was directed into the universe, uniting the early practitioners of magick with the primordial powers of the earth, and thus the eternal oracle was tapped. The Universal Mother and All Father archetypes transmitted the oracle's wisdom across space and time. Now, even as modern witchcraft begins to transcend the sexual polarity of male and female, Goddess and God, this unending flow of source energy still exists and is being discovered anew by witches.

# WHAT ARE RUNES?

When you think of runes, you usually think of a series of linear carvings. These are mainly associated with Scandinavia: Norway, Sweden, Denmark, and Iceland. As the Vikings spread their civilization across Europe, they brought runes with them. (Runes have been found as far away as Istanbul, where a couple of Vikings carved them into a stone rail in the great Hagia Sophia.) Scholars generally agree that early runic carvings date back to the first century, while some theorize that runes emerged during the third century. But what do runes have to do with magick? The answer to this question lies largely in the association runes have with mystery.

For witches, runes are basically four things: They are part language, part symbol, part oracle, and part talisman. Just as runes are many things at once, so are witches. Witches can be occultists or healers. They may practice spells and charms or enact ceremonial rituals. Some practice witchcraft as a religion, while others describe it as a path.

---

### The Number Four

The number four frequently comes up in witchcraft. When casting a circle, spiritual witches will turn to the four directions and call upon the spirits who dwell within the realms of points on the compass rose to enter into their sacred space. On the altar, there are usually representations of the four elements frequently used in witchcraft: air, fire, water, and earth. Witches may invoke a Triple Goddess and a God—making four in total. They may acknowledge four ancient fire festivals or four cross-quarter days and four points of seasonal change.

---

In addition to religious witches and secular witches, there is also a group of witches who claim witch and witchcraft as an identity but not as a practice. Some witches honor a Goddess and a God, while others do not; however, nearly all witches engage with some sort of divination technique.

---

### Gender Identity

In exploring the magickal and mystical realm of runes, it is not necessary to have a fixed or gendered system of divination, nor is gender necessarily an entry point into any sort of magick, even as many will claim that runes carry with them a decidedly masculine energy.

---

*The Modern Witchcraft Guide to Runes*

Linguistically, runes appear to have been used as an ancient alphabet by people who otherwise did not leave much in the way of written texts behind. Some runic artifacts have been deciphered and translated, while others defy any sort of interpretation. This is part of the reason why runes and runic language are so mysterious. There aren't accompanying texts from antiquity that describe their meaning or use. Anthropologists, archaeologists, and scholars have made discoveries and connections about how they believe runes were originally used, but there is no direct evidence that confirms the many different hypotheses surrounding runes and rune lore. In fact, there are different rune systems that appear to be linked, but in actuality, they originate from different populations and represent different linguistic attributes.

## Runes As Language

Runes played an important role in the evolution of writing. Writing is a technology, a symbol of an advanced civilization. Systems of writing are influenced by many factors, such as the religious practices of the population, the political structure of the society, and the cultural values of the people. The earliest systems of writing originated in Mesopotamia. It is interesting to note that as the written word came into being, it was ushered in to human consciousness by Goddess-worshipping, polytheistic civilizations. Sumerian and Akkadian cuneiform are the earliest known systems of writing. The pictographic beauty of Egyptian hieroglyphs, such as the rock of El-Khawy, which is believed to be around 5,200 years old, continues to inspire and captivate magick practitioners today. As trade routes became established and the migration of cultures became widespread, and as literacy came into being, language evolved and moved along with populations.

It has been conjectured that both the basic runic alphabet and the Ogham script, also called the Ogham runes, were inspired and influenced by trade and cultural exchange between the Romans, Celts, and Norse. The Theban runes are also connected through the Roman Empire. Tracing the history of runes is akin to tracing the footsteps of humanity across the planet through time as literacy spread across the earth.

Early systems of writing were local. In both eastern and western Europe, the dominant influence on literacy was clearly religion. Literacy was always the domain of spiritually minded people. As writing moved from pictographic forms to alphabetic ones, it also became standardized, and communication was transformed.

---

### The Distant Past Informs the Present

Written language first appeared as hieroglyphs and cuneiform. Ancient civilizations sought to create enduring communication through pictographic representations, which were then associated with sounds. The sounds were given unique characters, and written communication moved away from representative form into the lexical and literal characters that we use today.

With the advent of smartphones and digital communications, there has been a shift back to pictographic communication as emojis replace words. They communicate complex emotions, states of wellness or illness, activities, and all the accoutrements of daily life as well as the cosmos. In a sense, emojis are similar to hieroglyphs and are used in witchcraft to communicate everything from the phase of the moon to astrological signs. The past is constantly emerging, for the spiral of time never ceases.

---

It is interesting to note that the earliest alphabetic writings were spiritual—either pre-Christian or biblical—in nature. There has always been a desire among people to connect with their spirituality and communicate it through the written word.

Early writing systems, such as Phoenician, influenced other written languages, including archaic Greek, Anatolian, Balkan, Aramaic, and Hebrew. As alphabetic writing spread geographically, it also changed. Language systems evolved and developed into distinct scripts as they passed from place to place. Phoenician influenced the Punic script and the Greek alphabet in the West, and the Greek and Etruscan alphabets informed the Roman, or Latin, alphabet. There are strong visual similarities between the patterns of script in early alphabetic languages from Greece and Italy and Germanic runes. While the exact dates and methods of transmission of written language from East to West to North can never be definitively known, adaptation and cooperation among cultures allowed for sounds and symbols to combine and connect, to strengthen communication, and to record and reveal secrets.

As Germanic tribes expanded in both population and geography, the historical importance of the Goths, one of the main Germanic tribes, increased. Gothic language is significant because the few known runic Gothic inscriptions appear to predate the Germanic language by around four hundred years. The two Gothic dialects died out after the fall of their kingdom, which once stretched from eastern Europe to Italy. This conceivably makes Gothic runes a precursor to Germanic runes. Although there are very few surviving manuscripts from the earliest centuries of our common era, the Germanic runes have endured, along with their associations with supernatural powers. While the Gothic language has died out, the fascination with and modern use of runes remains.

Some scholars vehemently insist that any exploration of runes as a source of divine or metaphysical power is inappropriate and vulgar. To do so ignores the fact that the dissemination of spiritual beliefs has always been a central reason for the existence of the written word itself. In exploring the etymological origins of the word "rune," we should not be dismissive of mystical implications and associations. The connection between runes and mystery transcends the barriers of language and translation. The Greek translation connects *runa mysterion* to both "mystery" and "secret," while Old English, Old Norse, and Old High German all bear meanings that include "whisper," "secret," and "private counsel."

### Runes As Symbol

Runes have phonetic equivalences—that is, they have unique sound signatures that allow them to be pronounced, combined, and spoken, and specific sounds are represented by individual symbols, which are usually but not always a configuration of diagonal lines along a vertical stave. Runes that are linked together are bindrunes; they can represent morphemes, which are parts of words, or entire words themselves.

The spoken word is heard and felt, both audibly and emotionally. It is a vibrational energy born through breath and vibration within the body and then projected outward, creating a resonance that can be shared, heard, and interpreted by others. Spoken words carry great power, and it is a radical act to speak an intention or desire out loud. The simple act of speaking imbues any magickal work, ritual, or spell with power. Runes are an ideal medium for expressing the most secret of desires, those events we most want to call into being, or the quiet, hidden parts of ourselves most in need of healing.

Few things compare with the power of the spoken word when it comes to effecting change. Spoken words hold us accountable to our communities. They are the outward expression of our inner lives: our hopes, dreams, desires, ethics, and beliefs. To be characterized as "a person of your word" means that you are trusted and respected. Prayers are often spoken aloud and in unison, making runes a suitable vehicle for raising and directing energy in group work or coven craft. Imagine the ability to write a spell to bring about a desired outcome in a secret language that can be spoken aloud and understood only by those on the same or similar path. The possibilities for empowerment and actualization are tantalizing, and runes provide a powerful gateway into one of the most magickal forms of human expression.

As surprising as it may be to many, just as a magickal practice cannot be spiritually separated from the person who practices it, likewise, metaphysical and occult experiences do not require any external "belief" to make them valid. The forces of nature exist whether or not you have direct observation or experience of them; if you don't see them, it doesn't mean they don't occur. The answer to the old philosophical question, "If a tree falls in a forest, and no one is around to hear it, does it make a sound?" of course is "yes." The vibration is released whether or not anyone is present to observe it. The resonance of sound travels whether or not you hear it or acknowledge it.

To assume that your observation of an event is the only criterion that establishes existence is to greatly exaggerate your role as observer. Whether or not you believe in the power of runes and the augmented energy of the spoken word, this power still exists. Runes do not require your belief in them in order to retain their power; however, whenever you engage with any magickal practice, there is some kind of change that always takes place. Your mere presence has an impact on an occurrence. Even particles of light have been noticed to behave differently under an observational eye.

The issue of perception is an important one. As your perception grows, so does your acceptance of the unexplainable. Acceptance of the undecipherable is a desirable characteristic when engaging with the enigmatic energy of runes. You'll find a suspension of disbelief is useful in maintaining an open mind when working with runes. Be open to what the runes show you, especially if these things cannot be easily explained.

## Runes As Oracle

Runes are a link between the natural world and human agency that the modern witch is meant to decipher, interpret, and use. Runes continue to be spoken in secret by the modern keepers of the old ways, whether anyone believes in their power or not.

Of course, manifestations and affirmations are immensely encouraging. Signs that let you know you are on the right path, that petitions are being fulfilled, are satisfying. Successes will often lead to greater successes, and when you formulate an intention with clarity, direct it with focus, and project it into the world or universe, then its energy signature will continue whether anyone else believes in it or not.

This is important to understand, because in the phonetic study of runes, you aren't going to find a lot of reassurance that you're using them "correctly." It is a wonder of the age and the blessing of the modern witch that allows us unprecedented access to the mysteries of the past and the powerful acceptance of our own ability to synthesize the past into something relevant, vital, and necessary today. While modern witches practice within the context of a world that our forebears could not have possibly imagined, the technology of writing and its union with the spoken word transcends time.

## Runes As Talisman

Runes—and objects decorated with runes—have served as talismans used by witches in casting spells and divination. Runes are always associated with mystery. In addition to being an alphabetic system of writing as well as a spoken, phonetic expression of language, runes exist as symbols. The time from the late Iron Age through the Middle Ages when runes first developed was a period of great innovation, as technological advances in metalworking and woodworking paved the way for even greater advances, such as shipbuilding. Newly built sailing vessels possessed greater maneuverability and were capable of sailing in the direction from which the wind was originating, thus allowing for more exploration, more trade, expanded cultural exchange, and, for better or worse, colonization and conquest.

Detailed drawings from the book *De Re Metallica* by the German scientist and scholar Georgius Agricola (1494–1555), which was published after his death, indicate that mining for metal had been around for quite some time and that Saxon mines were a carefully regulated enterprise. Methods of mining for ore, smelting, and fabrication are described and illustrated along with geologic information that suggests these technologies were in use long before Agricola recorded them.

---

### Agricola's Many Facets

Agricola was known as a progenitor of mineralogy and was also acclaimed as a physician; he is credited with introducing the practice of quarantine, which is still in wide use today.

---

In the past, runes were used to inscribe specific pleas to ward off disease, a magickal practice with practical implications today. Creating a bindrune for health won't repel a rapidly mutating virus, but it will help you center your mind and your behavior with the intention of avoiding exposure. In this sense, the modern use of runes mirrors the past.

Runes and runic writings from the first century to the Middle Ages were scratched, carved, or engraved on objects. Most surviving runes were carved into stones, and "carved in stone" has become an adage to describe things that are permanent, unchangeable, and irrefutable. Such is the enduring power of runes. Runes were also inscribed in metal objects of great variety. In addition to a system of writing, they also seem to have been a method of decoration and adornment. Not all early examples of runic writing can be translated. Runes were more than a way to distinguish ownership or to impart a sentiment. These symbols clearly had a meaning and purpose that went beyond words.

Just as magick cannot be separated from the practitioner, runes cannot be separated from the objects upon which they are inscribed. Runes were used not only to show ownership but also to protect, to ward off evil, to quell storms, and to allow for safe passages to unknown lands. The spells written in runes called for abundant catches of fish and bountiful harvests, and they served as a link between the petition and the petitioner. Whether runes were employed to appeal to one God or to many Gods, there is power in the runes themselves.

---

### Runa Mysterion

The magickal and mysterious associations with runes date back to the earliest appearances of the word and its Greek translation. The Greek word *mysterion* was synonymous with "rune." Runes were used in the description of religious mystery cults and implied hidden realities that were accessible only to initiates. Laypeople required parables or other symbolic explanations, while initiates possessed secret knowledge. Words such as *mysterion*, *runa*, and *garuni* referred to rites of passage or holy mysteries. In the Gothic translation of the Bible by Ulfilas (311–382), there are several instances of equivalence of meaning between *mysterion* and "rune."

---

# WHY SHOULD YOU USE RUNES?

More than a mystery, runes carry with them the potential for the manifestation of wisdom. Magick practitioners of all kinds consult a variety of oracles in order to divine information from a realm beyond the everyday. Witches are open-minded and tend to be more accepting of unexplained phenomena than non-magickal people. While some witches engage in their craft in practical activities (through herbs they grow, foods they prepare, healings they undertake, and seasonal and celestial events they acknowledge), they do not necessarily link these to their spirituality. For others, witchcraft is a deeply spiritual path filled with reverent devotion and awe and is directly influenced and impacted by communion with and awareness of divine entities.

Runes are accessible to both types of modern witches because whether or not a higher power is invoked, the power and mystery of the runes endure. Because they were used in a variety of ways, sometimes in ways that defy any interpretation, using runes can be a liberating experience for the modern witch. They are free to engage in practices with runes that may include consecration, delineating ownership, imbuing objects with power, or pure adornment.

## Improving Self-Awareness

In addition to character and sound, runes have individual meanings that were given to them by early people; yet the further we get from the past, the more we realize that the threads that connect humanity throughout time, the issues that human beings ceaselessly grapple with, remain largely unchanged spiritually. Technology and locations may change, but our emotional needs endure. Like a wise and knowing disembodied voice from another time, the language of the runes speaks to our hearts.

Reading runes requires a certain level of self-examination. In times of struggle, when difficulties arise and confidences must be kept, consulting the runes is always safe. Runes are finite and infinite. This dichotomy is possible because although an alphabet may end, there are seemingly unlimited combinations that can be created by combining letters and sounds. Language by its very nature is, and has always been, a mutable process. Meaning evolves and changes over time, just as people do. When runes are incorporated into a magickal or spiritual path, life changes become more apparent because they are noticed. In this seeking, there is a natural instinct to record. Recording rune spreads—the configuration or order in which you select your runes and the associated meanings of the specific placements of each rune—allows the practitioner to look back, contemplate, revisit lessons, learn, let go, and move on. Runes are a powerful instrument of growth.

## Receiving Messages Through Divination

Divination is considered a magickal art. You open your mind to the point where it is capable of both generating and receiving thoughts. This receptive state allows you to interpret messages, thoughts, and guidance as well as wisdom and portents of things that are likely to occur. When a thought is formed, electrical synapses fire along a sequence of established pathways in the brain. Divination involves a similar process, yet the *origin* of the idea, message, or teaching is channeled from energy generated from an outside source, which is interpreted by the individual, and then communicated.

For spiritual witches, divination is considered a communion with deity. Wisdom gained and oracles channeled are based on a relationship between a Goddess or God and the devotee. Secular witches do not subscribe to such a relationship; instead, they either consider themselves to be the generators, or source, of the message or they believe that the wisdom is inherent to the transmission method itself, such as runes. Divination is not unlike mediumship, where communication is conveyed from a discarnate spirit to an incarnate spirit, but instead of a discarnate spirit who may make their previous incarnation known, the oracle comes from a place of mystery. If you have ever wanted to have a conversation with someone who has passed on, then you understand the draw of divination. There is a separation between the material, physical world and the spiritual realms. Runes are a gateway between these worlds. They serve as a portal between the seeker and the mystery.

## Spellcasting with Runes

Spellcasting is the combination of words and actions paired with a specific intention that is directed toward a power or source point in order to elicit a series of controlled coincidences; these, in turn, lead to a desired result.

---

### Controlled Coincidences

A controlled coincidence happens when the very thing you wish to happen occurs in a natural way that may at first seem unconnected to your initial spell. For example, you may cast a prosperity spell and shortly thereafter discover that someone has spontaneously decided to repay you for an old debt. You put an intention into the universe. Your request was granted via an apparent coincidence that was in direct alignment with your wish.

---

Incorporating runes into spellcasting is feasible because runes already exist in the triple form of symbol, word, and deed that comprises the elemental necessity for successful spells. They represent speech, action, and talismans (charms).

For example, a word or desire spoken aloud in and of itself is not a spell. It could be a petition, a prayer, or a request, but it is not a spell. It is only one part of a spell. Runes can be pronounced and spoken aloud, so they have the ability to fulfill the speech part of a spell. A spell also requires action on the part of the practitioner. There is something you are called to do, change, or affect in some way. The act of scribing a rune is an action. It aligns deed with word, so runes fulfill the action part of spellcasting as well. Finally, spells will usually involve talismans. In order to scribe a rune, an object must be used. No matter what medium you decide to work with—paper, stone, wax, or some other substance—the object that is scribed with intention and marked in runes becomes a talisman in its own right. Thus, the word is combined with action and bound to object. This practice is time-honored, relevant, empowering, and effective.

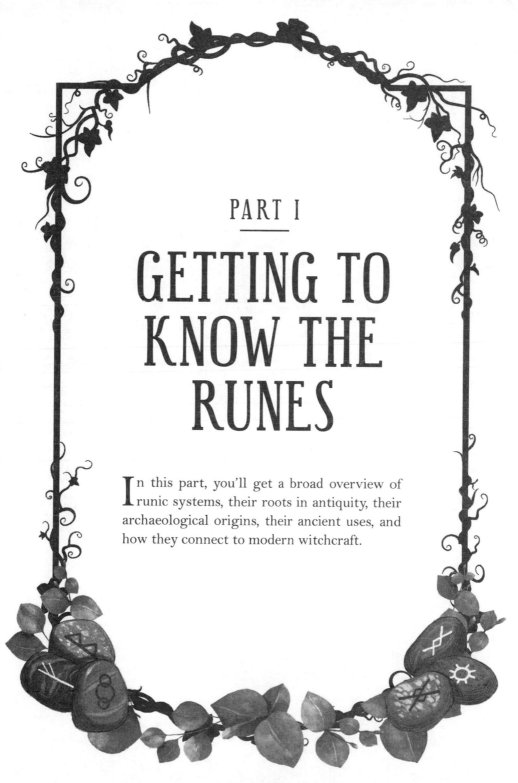

# PART I
---

# GETTING TO KNOW THE RUNES

In this part, you'll get a broad overview of runic systems, their roots in antiquity, their archaeological origins, their ancient uses, and how they connect to modern witchcraft.

# Chapter 2

# NORSE/GERMANIC/ VIKING RUNES: ELDER AND YOUNGER FUTHARK

lso known as Viking runes, the Elder and Younger Futhark are sometimes referred to as the Elder and Younger Rune Row. The term "Futhark" refers to the first five characters of the alphabetic system that consisted of twenty-four characters in the "Elder" Rune Row. This was subsequently shortened to sixteen characters, the "Younger" Futhark. Each symbol has its own unique name and sound.

The reduction in the number of runes from the Elder to the Younger is curious and largely unexplained. As runes were combined, they disappeared for unknown reasons. There is much to be learned from this ensuing mystery. To begin unraveling the enigma of runes, it is helpful to engage with several disciplines, including archaeology, philology, linguistics, and occultism.

# HISTORY OF ELDER AND YOUNGER FUTHARK

*The Poetic Edda* is believed to have been written around 1200. This collection of Old Norse poems by an unknown author gives us great insight into the culture and customs of northern European life and provides context for the significance of runes. Included in *The Poetic Edda* is a verse known as the *Hávamál* ("Words of the High One"), which legend holds to be the words of the Norse God, Odin. In the *Hávamál*, there are direct references to the runes that connect them to Odin and to their power and magickal purpose:

> "NOW IS ANSWERED WHAT YOU ASK OF THE RUNES,
> GRAVEN BY THE GODS, MADE BY THE ALL FATHER,
> SENT BY THE POWERFUL SAGE..."

Runes are explicitly described as a language, for the *Hávamál* also states:

> "LONG I LISTENED TO MEN
> RUNES HEARD SPOKEN (COUNSELS REVEALED)..."

The poem reveals how Odin underwent an ordeal and pain to learn the mystery of the runes. To understand the significance of the connection between runes and spirit, it is important to have some knowledge of Odin.

# MASTER OF ECSTASY

There is no deity quite like Odin. He is enigmatic and complex. He bears the power and regality of Zeus as well as the wisdom and suffering of Christ. You would be hard-pressed to find a deity as all-encompassing and traditionally masculine as Odin. He is described as a formidable warrior, and in discovering the runes, he sacrificed his left eye in exchange for wisdom. He hung from Yggdrasil, the legendary "world tree," or tree of life, for nine days after he was pierced by a spear. With a tolerance for pain that made him unconquerable in battle as well as an intimate acquaintance with suffering, Odin is credited with bringing the runes to humankind. He did not write or invent the runes, according to *The Poetic Edda*. The lore explains that Odin, without food or drink or aid of any kind, hung in an inverted suspension between the worlds and brought the runes into the consciousness of his followers by being the first to see them.

Adding to the mystery is the fact that Odin was also considered a master of *seid*, a magickal power that manifests physically but is not limited to the earthly plane. *Seid* is a transcendent, feminine form of ecstatic magick, and some scholars have implied that the masculine God Odin may have taken on a female form in order to learn it.

---

### *Seid* and *Sorcery*

While segments of the three major culturally dominant Abrahamic religions of today emphasize asceticism, this was not the norm in times past. *Seid* was an ecstatic form of magick, quite the opposite of abstinence and the denial of pleasure. *Seid* was a decidedly feminine type of magick in which the song (*vardlokkur*) is sung to summon spirit guides who enable the sorceress to see the future. This is described in the Old Norse saga of Erik the Red. Scholars have suggested that Odin's mastery of *seid* indicates some level of gender fluidity.

---

# A BRIEF HISTORY OF RUNOLOGY

Runology, the systematic study of runes, is credited to Johannes Bureus (1568–1652), who was a member of the Swedish court and was the first to theorize that runes held mystic significance as receptacles of ancient wisdom that transcended their conventional alphabetic meanings. Bureus is described as a Christian, yet his own beliefs did not preclude him from attributing the runes with mystical characteristics. This is important to note because modern scholars often imply it is wrong to associate runes with more than letters and sounds. However, such an approach discounts a substantial part of the nature of runes.

Although the use of runes as both a writing system and as a spoken language had died out by the late Middle Ages, their relevance and importance remained. By the mid-nineteenth century, runology as a branch of academic study was solidified. Like the runes themselves, which exist as many things at once—symbol, sound, object, and oracle—runology is a multidisciplinary group of academic disciplines, including linguistics, archaeology, anthropology, and philology.

### The Rök Runestone

Most of the runic carvings that have survived to this day are found in Sweden. One of the most significant discoveries in rune lore is the Rök Runestone, which was carved around C.E 800. A recent interpretation of the runic carvings on the Rök Runestone reveals an epic story of the death of the Sun Goddess, slain by a great wolf. Odin calls mankind into battle to avenge her death. This interpretation of the inscription connects mythology and legend to the devastating effects of climate change, an enduring issue we still grapple with to this day.

The story of the death of the Sun Goddess corresponds with a volcanic eruption in C.E. 536 so powerful that it interfered with the light of the sun for over a decade. The battle of mankind against the great wolf was the mythic response of a people devastated by climate change, who were enduring an environmental event of catastrophic proportions. Restoring hope to humanity, a new Goddess arose to replace her mother, and this miraculous resolution of an actual disaster is described in a series of ciphers that have endured for ages.

### The Kylver Stone

There are over four hundred known examples of the Futhark alphabet, and one of the best and earliest is the Kylver Stone in Gotland, Sweden. This fifth-century carving contains the entire sequence of the Elder Rune Row.

# THE NORSE RUNE ALPHABETS: MEANING, SYMBOLISM, AND PRONUNCIATION

Runes are read from right to left, and each rune has a distinct shape or character, a phonetic value or sound, a name, and a meaning or association. As language evolved, variations emerged; however, the Elder Futhark Rune Row is generally accepted as follows:

| Number | Sound | Name | Meaning |
|--------|-------|------|---------|
| 1 | F | Fehu | Livestock |
| 2 | U | Uruz | Aurochs |
| 3 | Th | Thurisaz | Giant |
| 4 | A | Ansuz | The God |
| 5 | R | Raidō | Riding |
| 6 | K | Kaunaz | Sore |
| 7 | G | Gebō | Gift |
| 8 | W | Wunjō | Joy |
| 9 | H | Hagalaz | Hail |
| 10 | N | Nauthiz | Need |
| 11 | I | Isa | Ice |
| 12 | J | Jēra | Year |
| 13 | Ei | Eihaw | Yew |
| 14 | P | Perthro | Dicebox |
| 15 | Z | Elhaz | Elk |
| 16 | S | Sowilo | Sun |
| 17 | T | Teiwaz | Tyr |
| 18 | B | Berkanō | Birch |
| 19 | E | Ehwaz | Horse |
| 20 | M | Mannaz | Self |
| 21 | L | Laguz | Water |
| 22 | Ng | Ingwaz | Yngvi |
| 23 | D | Dagaz | Day |
| 24 | O | Ōthala | Ancestral estate |

Language is never fixed—in fact, it constantly changes. In addition, phonetics and dialects of language impact how we hear and interpret sounds, so for those reasons, you will find many variations on how the names of these runes are spelled.

# MODERN EQUIVALENCES OF ANCIENT RUNES

Just as language has evolved over time, so have the mystical associations with runes. Runes speak to the human experience across the ages, but they have modern relevance as well. Runes are tied not only to the daily lives and activities of the ancient people who first used them—they also hold significance in their universal connections to common threads of the desires and dangers that people face today.

## *Fehu*

Fehu represents livestock. Long before the existence of large-scale factory farms, animal husbandry and the raising of livestock was equated with social status, wealth, and the ability to provide for one's family. Fehu is a rune of ability and comfort. It represents wealth, stature, and success. Fehu indicates a favorable situation. It also represents how we are seen by others. The external energy of this rune is one of respect and achievement. Internally, it is accomplishment and success.

## *Uruz*

Uruz represents aurochs, a species of cattle inhabiting Europe. Throughout many civilizations and systems of both belief and myth, the image of the sacred bull is a recurring symbol. Uruz is a rune of power and strength, fortitude, respect, and awe. Uruz represents the power of the Gods and the necessity for sacrifice. It is a symbol of strength, stamina, and endurance.

## Thurisaz

Thurisaz refers to the God Thor and to giants. This is the rune of the gateway, the obstacles that threaten to obstruct movement. It is the standstill before the gate can be passed, before progress is to be made. Thurisaz indicates that an opening or opportunity is near. It is a rune of patience and waiting. The wisdom of Thurisaz knows the difference between when to take action and when to lie in wait. Thurisaz is the stillness before the storm. It is a harbinger of significant things to come.

## Ansuz

Ansuz is associated with the God principle and is particularly connected to Loki, the trickster God. Ansuz is also considered a messenger rune. Think of the different ways that messages get to you and be on the lookout for the unexpected text as well as the unmistakable presence of intuition. This rune tells you an important message is at hand. Ansuz asks you to be wary and keep your wits about you and to pay close attention to communication channels.

## Raidō

Raidō is a rune of swift movement; it is action taken with speed. Originally it meant "riding," so Raidō can even signify a sudden change, travel, or possibly a move. With Raidō, whatever change is at hand will come quickly. Raidō encourages you to prepare quickly for a possibly wild ride.

## Kaunaz

Kaunaz is connected to fire and can signify the beginning of a process. Literal translations from different locales were varied in that Kaunaz was used to signify a torch or light, but also an ulcer or a sore. This can represent a new endeavor, a healing of an emotional wound, or a fresh start. Think of Kaunaz as the purification and preparation for great things to come. Kaunaz is a rune that calls for clearing an area. Examine the things that no longer serve you and consider letting them go.

## Gebō

Gebō is a gift. This can be something welcomed and unexpected coming into your life. It can also signify a healthy relationship or a balanced partnership. Gebō is a rune of manifesting and acknowledgment. It calls you to a profound place of happiness.

## Wunjō

Wunjō is a rune of joy, representing happiness and fulfillment. Connected to flowering fruit trees, this rune means attainment of your desire is at hand. Wunjō represents beauty, possibility, and that positive things are coming into being.

*Part I: Getting to Know the Runes*

# Hagalaz

Hagalaz signifies hail. Hail and dangerous weather conditions can indicate that change is at hand and that you must remain open and tenacious and ready to deal with whatever life may throw you. Hagalaz calls upon you to protect yourself from things that are beyond your control. It may indicate that an unsafe situation is approaching.

# Nauthiz

Nauthiz is the rune of need. Necessary things are always difficult to bear. This is a rune of responsibility and reckoning. Nauthiz calls you to persevere and shoulder your burdens. It represents a time to examine and identify the things that you are lacking.

# Isa

Isa is the rune of ice. It represents immobility or a standstill. Drawing Isa indicates that you may quite literally feel frozen and unable to enact a change or that there will be a delay or postponement of plans. Isa may remind you to slow down or stop what you are doing altogether.

## Jēra

This rune is connected to harvest and can signify one year's time. The fulfillment of any endeavor will not be swift, but it will come in its due time. Jēra is a rune of sowing, tending, waiting, and, finally, gathering. Jēra means that patience is required and that rewards will come to you after the work has been completed, but not before. It is a rune of faith and trusting that things will unfold based on what you have already invested.

## Eihaw

Signifying the yew tree, which is considered sacred to the dead, Eihaw is a rune of remembrance. Eihaw gives you room to grieve and remember. It can signify someone who has moved on to the spirit world but remains close. Eihaw may indicate that your ancestors are drawing near. Remember that in sadness and times of loss, there is also love that remains.

## Perthro

Perthro is chance, fate, and risk. Whether the outcome is positive or negative, Perthro is a throw of the dice and reminds us that seemingly random events will ultimately connect us to fate. Perthro indicates the necessity to be both bold and wary, to balance risk and reward.

## Elhaz

Elhaz signifies elk. Elk were an important food source, so their modern equivalent would be material comfort and provisions as well as satisfaction of spiritual hunger. Elhaz is a rune of satiety, stability, and protection. When basic needs are met, a higher level of attainment can be achieved. Elhaz is a call to recognize your needs as an individual and to build strong foundations.

## Sowilo

Sowilo is the rune of the sun. This rune represents the life force, the balance of nature, the power of God, and literal enlightenment. Sowilo is a bright happiness that indicates successful endeavors. It permeates all things and is a very positive indicator that you will flourish.

## Teiwaz

Teiwaz, connected to the God Tyr, is also known as the warrior rune. Shaped like an arrow, Teiwaz emboldens us to powerfully move the trajectory of our lives with confidence and strength. It indicates the importance of cutting away and releasing that which no longer serves us. Teiwaz means that while success is at hand, most likely it will be hard-won. It is a call to focus.

## Berkanō

Berkanō represents the birch tree, one of the nine sacred woods of witchcraft. It is considered taboo to burn the wood of the birch tree. Berkanō is a rune of respect and boundaries, wisdom and growth. Expect positive changes and the benefits of lessons learned to manifest.

## Ehwaz

Ehwaz is the horse rune. To master the horse was to master your destiny, to be successful in battle, and to prevail in the face of adversity. Ehwaz represents triumph and freedom, exploration and movement. It may represent a confident and accomplished person, secure in their abilities.

## Mannaz

Mannaz represents the self. Mannaz calls us to focus on individual needs so that we can better participate in the whole of humanity. Before enacting meaningful change in the world, we must first become better stewards of ourselves. Mannaz is a call to self-care and inward reflection so that we can authentically connect with others. Self-awareness is different from self-centeredness. Mannaz demands that the self be honored in relation to others. Clarification of relationships may be at hand.

## Laguz

Laguz is the rune of water. Signifying flow, Laguz instructs us to let go and let the currents take us to our next destination. Laguz requires a certain amount of trust and release. Going with the flow can be a challenge, but it leads to a realm of peace. Laguz is a rune of acceptance and movement, as well as allowance for outside forces to assist in moving the questioner in the direction they need to go.

## Ingwaz

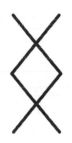

Ingwaz is named for Yngvi, God of heroes. Ingwaz is indicative of a new beginning, a fresh start, or an emergence from a difficult period. The challenge is behind you and something new awaits. Step into a new realm of being with Ingwaz as your guide. Victory or overcoming an obstacle is at hand.

## Dagaz

*Dagaz* means "day." It is the rune of breakthroughs and new chapters unfolding. As the dawn of the sun pierces the darkness and ends the night, Dagaz call us to move into bright new endeavors with confidence. It may signify that an old paradigm is dismantled to make room for a new level of understanding. It is a fresh start, enlivening and inspiring. Rise to a new level of awareness. Dagaz is a rune of growth and advancement.

## Ōthala

Ōthala is the rune of the ancestral estate. It requires us to examine our roots, honor our ancestors and all our relations, and confront and heal generational wounds. Ōthala is a rune signifying a great span of time or a situation that has evolved over many generations. It may represent ingrained patterns, or traditions and long-held beliefs.

# USES OF RUNES, THEN AND NOW

Aside from recording historical or poetic tracts, runes were used for many magickal reasons, such as influencing the weather, receiving protection in battle, harvesting abundant crops, attracting love, grieving death, affecting the tides, and ensuring safe travels. Since many of the original uses of runes were to bless, honor, and protect people, things, and places from all manner of environmental impacts and attacks from enemies, and also to indicate affection, relationship, and possession, it is entirely feasible to craft a modern runic tradition. In truth, much of the human condition remains largely unchanged. We still grapple with climate change. We still experience change and loss. We still want to ward off pandemics. We still seek to protect our beloveds and our belongings. We continue to seek love. In these pursuits, runes can be valuable tools.

An issue that does bear examining is how to reconcile the power of runes with the danger you may encounter when reinterpreting an ancient system for modern use. Since it is not possible to truly know the intentions of the original rune-masters, what is the modern witch to make of the recent resurgence of interest in runes as emblems of power and domination over others?

People across the globe struggle with how to categorize and integrate groups of people who do not conform to the false reality of societally acceptable views and lifestyles. People with non-conforming identities, such as "witch," can have a hard time fitting in. Runes have been used as symbols of power, and some suggest that this system is not or should not be available to all people. For witches, this is a particularly acute problem. Witches have always been outsiders. The role of the witch in society has often been that of scapegoat; they've been held responsible for crop failures, the deaths of livestock, and other maladies. Today, that mindset persists, albeit in different forms.

To believe or enforce the domination of one group of people over another is antithetical to a moral magickal practice. To close yourself off from the collective culture of humanity is to deny the acquisition and dissemination of wisdom. As a practitioner of magick, you must approach runes with an awareness of the sacredness and validity of all beings. This is a key element to successful divination.

# THE YOUNGER RUNE ROW

While it may seem somewhat paradoxical, as language became more complex and more phonetic combinations came into wider use, the Elder Rune Row was shortened from twenty-four characters to sixteen. This transition occurred during the dawn of the Viking age around the tenth century. The Younger Rune Row uses only four vowel sounds and eliminates eight runes from the Elder Futhark Rune Row. The Elhaz rune, representing the "z" sound, appears in the Younger Rune Row, but it is inverted. This is one of several differences between the Elder and Younger Rune Rows.

Other names for the Younger Futhark include the "staveless" runes and the "long branch" runes. This is because the Younger system is simplified not only in number but also in form. Each character has a single vertical stave (line), which means they could be carved easily and quickly. Each character has curved or crossed lines that offshoot or intersect the vertical stave. While, like the Elder Futhark (also called the Elder Rune Row and the Norse runes), the Younger Rune Row (also called the Younger Futhark) is divided into families called *ættir*, the two rune systems differ in their economy. Because it is more concise, the Younger Futhark contains fewer characters, so a single character represents more than one sound.

## Making Sense of Their Many Names

There are several variations of the Elder and Younger names used—for example, Younger Rune Row, Younger Futhark, Elder Rune Row, and Elder Futhark Rune Row. All of these names are widely used and generally understood to reference the same sets of characters. It is reminiscent of how some people describe the United States as America, the United States, the United States of America, and the USA.

Another variation of the Younger Futhark is the short twig runes, which resemble script. "Short twig" is a Scandinavian term, while "long branch" is Danish. The Younger Futhark runes continued to evolve; inscriptions with dotted characters have been discovered, possibly indicating variations in sound. Additionally, it was not unheard of for Latin phrases to appear carved in Scandinavian runes. As explorers moved across the seas, they brought their language and writing systems with them, and variations of runes began to populate beyond the borders of their country of origin. No longer limited to Scandinavia, runes made their way to the Isle of Man in the Irish Sea, and syncretism—the merging of different inflections of a word—began to take root as variations of the Younger Futhark were blended together.

Eventually, the Younger Futhark runes were simplified further into what are known as the staveless runes. It is fascinating to contemplate the changes that occurred to runes across countries and centuries, especially because the evolution is counterintuitive. You might think that an alphabetic system would grow in its number and in its complexity of character, but in studying runes, you will find that the opposite is true. The runes got smaller and ever more simplified until they fell out of common use.

# RUNE SPREADS

A rune spread is a focused interpretation of certain runes in a specific order. Rune spreads can be as simple or as complex as your needs. Whether you need a quick check-in or a read on a situation, even an in-depth examination of a question from many angles, there are a variety of spreads you can use with Norse runes. While the runes of focus and the order in which they are contemplated are selected at random, each individual selection and the order in which the runes are selected are distinct and carry significance.

Begin by formulating a question in your mind. The question should be specific to a situation for which more information is required. Furthermore, the question should be open-ended, without a clear yes or no answer. The question should also directly address the oracle, meaning that you are seeking an answer from a source of power, not just wondering or wishing. When using runes for divination, you are asking magickal tools to serve as a conduit between yourself and information you need.

---

### Have Joy in Your Heart

Requests are made with seriousness, although seriousness does not mean without levity. You can ask a serious question with joy in your heart. Runes transcend time and are intimately connected to almost every level of the human experience; therefore, it is only natural to approach them with respect to their enduring power, no matter what the disposition of the questioner may be.

---

# SINGLE-RUNE SPREAD

The simplest way to engage with runes is with a single-rune spread. Modern runes used for divination come in many forms, from small tiles of ceramic, wood, or metal to tumbled gemstones or even sticks and dice. For the single-rune spread, allow yourself a moment of stillness. Turn off your phone. Eliminate distractions. If you already have your own set of runes, either on tiles, sticks, or stones, gather them together in a pouch or place them facedown in a single layer. Before you select a rune, formulate the question in your mind. When your question is clear, speak it aloud over the runes and see to which rune you are drawn by choosing one without looking. Some suggestions on how to formulate your question include beginning with the following thoughts:

- What are the influences surrounding you (an interpersonal relationship, a life decision, a current project or class, a career choice, etc.)?
- What is the best possible outcome to the current decision you are facing (your next steps, the options that have been presented, etc.)?
- What should you be focusing on in the coming week?
- What is stopping you from moving forward?

As you practice, your question formulation technique will become more refined. The guidance that you receive from consulting runes will have an impact on the way you frame your questions. Eventually, your ability to both ask and receive answers, as well as interpret those answers, will grow.

Now that your question is clear and you have established a desire to seek in your mind, you must speak the question aloud. This creates a vibration over the runes and will aid you in choosing the appropriate response. Choose a single rune and contemplate its meaning in relation to your question. Did you choose Laguz? It is time to go with the flow and allow things to unfold. Were you drawn to Isa? It's definitely time to hit pause and not make any sudden moves. Did you draw Raidō? Proceed full speed ahead.

# THREE-RUNE SPREAD

When you need more in-depth information or guidance, you can progress to using more runes. For religious witches, the number three is often a reference to the Triple Goddess, the divine feminine in her aspects of Maiden, Mother, and Crone. Secular as well as spiritual witches will sometimes abide by the Law of Three, which means that any intention, spell, or other magickal working will be amplified and returned to the practitioner threefold. For some, the Law of Three serves as an impetus to stay away from baneful magick, discouraging hexing; however, many practitioners who identify as witches do not abide by the Law of Three and reject its ethical implications outright.

A three-rune spread is highly magickal, and its simplicity should not obscure that. Your question formulation will remain the same, but you will draw three runes by choosing them at random without looking at them first and then read them from right to left.

### *Rune 1, placed on the right:*

The first rune you choose represents you in this moment. It is your current state of questioning and will shed insight on what you need to hear about your current situation.

### *Rune 2, placed in the center:*

The second one represents your inner emotions. This rune reveals how you are feeling about your current state. The rune you draw will be the rune you should meditate on in order to get some clarity about your emotions and what impact they may be having.

### *Rune 3, placed on the left:*

The third represents the environmental or external influences on your question. The third rune will put you in touch with yourself while providing some context for those around you. It will help you access your true feelings while guiding your next steps. It allows you to have a glimpse of how you are seen by others, and you may find that it is very different from the other two.

---

### Record Your Spreads

If you feel that the runes you have drawn are not appropriate or relevant to the situation on which you have based your query, keep in mind that the runes are, by nature, mysterious. The outcomes and influences may reveal themselves to you in the near term. This is why it is a good idea to record your rune spreads, because what is not immediately apparent will make more sense to you after you have had some time to experience and understand their message.

---

A three-rune spread is appropriate when a moment of clarity is needed. It is a self-check that will give you information not only about what you are going through but also how you are being affected by others.

# FIVE-RUNE SPREAD

The number five is sacred to witches because it corresponds to the five points of the pentagram, which has many powerful magickal associations. As delineated in Leonardo da Vinci's *Vitruvian Man*, the five points of the pentagram represent the self and the mind-body-spirit connection that is manifested through the connection of the head to the extremities. It is also connected with the elemental powers used in witchcraft: earth, air, fire, water, and oil.

To begin a five-rune spread, start at the top, or the "head" position. The first rune you draw will represent you in your present situation. Moving sunwise (clockwise), your next rune, placed in the "left hand" position, indicates your area of focus, the obstacle or issue that you must take in hand. The third rune, or "left foot," represents the past or the events that brought you to your present situation. The fourth rune, the "right foot" position, is the next step you must take. The final rune, the "right hand" position, represents the future, or that which will be within reach in the near term.

# TEN-RUNE SPREAD

The ten-rune spread provides in-depth information and should be used when you have time to take a deep dive into your psyche. A ten-rune spread requires contemplation and synthesis, as you will be called upon to examine many parts of your question. Because it uses so many runes, placement and context become very important. With an in-depth spread such as this, you may want to use more than one set of runes. It can be helpful to see if patterns arise and if a single rune is drawn multiple times. Just as certain words will have multiples of the same letter, using more than one set of runes for a spread can provide more information about the context of the issue you are exploring.

The ten-rune spread is a pyramid shape. It begins with the three-rune spread and then provides an expansion or extension of the initial situation, the inner conflict or emotion, and the external or environmental influences. The three-rune spread becomes the row that is in the middle of the pyramid. It represents the present.

Underneath the three-rune spread, choose and lay out four more runes from right to left. These runes are the foundation and future and represent, in order, the distant-past influence, the recent-past influence, the near-future influence, and the far-future influence. You can interpret the foundation row to reveal where you came from, the most recent event that brought you to this point, what lies just around the corner, and what the far-reaching implications will be.

Above the three runes representing your present, lay out two runes, again placed from right to left. These are your guiding runes. The first represents your obstacle, and the second is the way to integrate, confront, or resolve the obstacle. The topmost and final rune will be the culmination or final outcome.

As you become familiar with and adept at working with the Norse runes, you may be inspired to learn more modern systems, such as the Witch runes. Persist in your journey, and more occult knowledge will become known to you. As your confidence grows, so too will your wisdom.

*Chapter 3*

# WITCH RUNES

itch runes are intriguing and entrancing. These symbols are more complex than stave runes such as the Norse and Ogham, both in form and appearance as well as in their symbolism. There are two systems of writing and divination strongly associated with witches: Witch runes and the Theban alphabet. In this chapter, you'll learn about both symbology and the use of a secret alphabet for spells and grimoires (sacred books, always secret, that are kept as records of magickal practice by an individual witch or shared only with coven members).

During the Dark Ages, the period known as the "Burning Times" (a term popularized by a 1990 Canadian documentary film on the feminist history of witchcraft), persecution and execution of not just actual witches, but any person found "guilty"—whether they were an actual practitioner or not—was normalized. As a reaction to the consequences of discovery, where an accusation was often enough to justify a guilty verdict, it became customary for modern witches to keep the names of coven members secret and to hide spells and charms from those unfamiliar with magickal work. Fear of discovery in the past was based in the very real possibility of persecution. Having esoteric symbols enabled witches to record their spells, rituals, and other activities and to communicate with coven members, maintaining records without exposing themselves or others. Think of these symbols and glyphs as secret passwords that protect and keep private all matters of magick. Their representation, meaning, and use have evolved over time and will continue to do so.

# WHERE DID WITCH RUNES COME FROM?

The modern Witch runes consist of thirteen pictographic symbols often painted or inscribed on a round tile or stone. While their exact origins are unknown, this system of folk magick was popularized in the 1970s, largely due to an article written by Dana Corby (this article was later turned into book format, called *The Witches' Runes*). Witch runes continued to gain attention and use through the end of the twentieth century after being featured in *A Witch's Runes* by Susan Sheppard. Some claim that the Witch runes come from eastern Europe, while others suggest northeastern Scotland; however, no definitive connection has been determined—which only adds to their mystery. They do bear some resemblance in form and motif to early carvings done by the Scottish Picts, who were known for painting their bodies.

Rudimentary and simple, Witch runes represent natural events as well as important tools and times of year that have significance in witchcraft. They bear some resemblance to many ancient and esoteric scripts, including the symbols and silhouettes found in Egyptian hieroglyphs and the sigil-like seals of Slavic light symbols, which Witch runes strongly resemble in design. Predating Christianity and steeped in mythology, these symbols represented the pagan deities worshipped by tribal people as well as planes of existence such as life, the afterlife, and the celestial realms.

Because they are small in number, Witch runes are generally used for casting spells, scribing candles, emblazoning charms, and drawing in grimoires to add context and embellishment to entries; however, they are also used in readings and psychometry—a form of extrasensory perception specific to getting information from objects—albeit in spreads less complex than Elder Futhark or

Ogham. There are thirteen characters in the system, one for each complete lunar month in the calendar year, and modern witches often perform rituals and spells on the full moon. Witch runes bear a strong resemblance to early Bronze Age carvings, as they contain simple pictorial symbols.

### Sun

The Sun represents light, attainment, power, joy, fulfillment, family, and success. A circle with eight extending rays, it bears a strong resemblance to the celestial object it represents. The Sun means that growth, happiness, and peace are at hand. The Sun is also a rune of strength and is connected to masculine mysteries.

### Moon

The Moon is associated with the feminine Goddess. The Moon represents mystery, magick, change, wisdom, and knowledge. It is a rune of enhancement, and it is frequently used to amplify spells and to add the power of Goddess energy.

### Flight

The rune for Flight is a trio of wyverns that resembles a flock of soaring birds. Flight indicates a magickal experience, spiritual awakening, psychic opening, or some other significant transformation. Flight can also signify an actual journey taken recently or about to commence.

## Rings

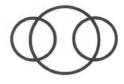

Depictions of the Rings vary. Sometimes they are rendered as two interlocking circles and sometimes as three. No matter the motif, the Rings are a symbol of a strong commitment. They represent a bond, which could mean a handfasting (a marriage) or a vow such as an engagement. The Rings also have a platonic aspect and can represent a meaningful promise or an important friendship.

## Man

Similar to Teiwaz, the warrior rune in the Elder Futhark, the Witch rune for Man could be considered a form of syncretism. This rune signifies a male person, which could be the self, a love interest, a possible father figure or authority figure, or the ancestral patrilineal line.

## Woman

The transcendent beauty of the female form is simply rendered on a forked stave. Resembling Baubo, an old woman who brought laughter to Demeter in her time of mourning for her daughter, the Woman rune can represent a female person or the self. Woman may symbolize a Goddess archetype, a love interest, a daughter, or a friend. When the Woman rune turns up in a "past" position in a reading (for example, a witch may perform a simple three-rune fortune-telling spread for "past," "present," and "future" with three runes drawn in that order), it may be a reference to the matrilineal line or a mother figure.

## Romance

A three-way motif composed of interlocking vesicae piscis, the rune of Romance means that love, sex, or marriage is the issue at hand. The Romance rune is also a symbol of partnership and companionship. The nature of the relationship is one of fidelity, honesty, and trust. A favorable influence, this rune may symbolize a deep friendship or a long-lasting, universal love. This rune is also used for fertility and sex magick.

## Harvest

For calling in wealth, acknowledging success, or amplifying abundance, Harvest is the rune of affluence. It signifies comfort, agency, and the ability to get things done. The Harvest rune is used for spells and rituals centered on prosperity, either your personal prosperity or in your outward or professional endeavors. Wealth represents different things to different people.

## Crossroads

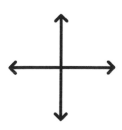

Represented by a pair of intersecting arrows, the Crossroads rune signifies that the time to make a choice is at hand. The Crossroads is also a harbinger of change. You may find yourself at a turning point or you may be asked to enter into a pact or some kind of agreement. This rune speaks of decisions for good or ill, and often with an accompanying sacrifice.

## Scythe

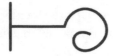

The breaking of bonds, endings of relationships, cord cutting, and disruption are all under the domain of the Scythe. The Scythe is not just used for separation. It is also potent for breaking hexes. The Scythe can also represent the time to take necessary action on releasing that which no longer serves you. Before the harvest is brought home, it must be cut. Before certain flowers will bloom, they need to be cut back. The Scythe calls to mind the necessary sacrifices that must be made in order to create space for good things to come.

## Wave

Spiraling scrolls ebb and flow in the rune for Wave. It is a rune of a change in circumstance. It is movement for better or worse and can signify an ambivalent disruption. The Wave heralds that a change is at hand, which may take the form of cleansing, releasing, and purity. This rune brings the opportunity to allow things to wash away. Waves are also powerful. They may knock you down, but the important thing is to face them and hold fast. The Wave calls upon you to gather your strength and face what is to come.

## Star

Four intersecting staves create the Star rune. Star is the rune of attainment and fulfillment. It is wishes and dreams granted. Since the Star is aligned with cosmic energy, meditating on it can produce a state of heightened awareness. For many, the Star is a symbol of a positive experience, good luck, and good fortune.

## *Eye*

Signifying an awakening, the Eye may also represent a sudden realization or the importance of trusting your intuition. It is a symbol of protection and can be used as a ward against enemies. The Eye represents psychic sight, visions, and even wariness.

### Secrecy and Witchcraft

The practice of witchcraft and its accompanying secrecy date back to ancient Mesopotamia. The earliest cuneiform tablets illustrate a society steeped in magick, which was practiced openly. Thirty percent of surviving cuneiform tablets make references to some type of incantation ranging from protection and fertility to wards, curses, and exorcisms.

While this openness may seem counterintuitive to the practice of secrecy, it is not entirely. Magick was a part of life and was seen as both beneficial and harmful. If someone suspected that evil had been done to them by a malevolent witch, the spell to reverse the damage involved the creation of nameless effigies, which were then burned. It is interesting to note the anonymity of the recipient of a counter-curse; the practitioner had an established relationship to the deities and trusted that the hand of divinity would deliver the correct level of restraint to the correct person.

Cuneiform clay tablets reveal a rich tradition of working relationships among Gods, Goddesses, spirits—both good and bad—and people. For many witches, the same energetic principles that govern these relationships still exist today. While language and literacy have evolved over eras and epochs, the need of the individual to become adept at magick has remained largely unchanged. Witches still seek communion, communication, and guidance. They still look to the stars, the phases of the moon, the flower, leaf, and root for pathways into source energy.

# WHY USE WITCH RUNES?

Witch runes are esoteric, beautiful, and among the most modern of occult motifs. Their simple forms and direct implications make them easy to understand. Like the Elder and Younger Futhark runes, they are versatile and can be drawn on paper, which can be folded into charms or rolled and placed in witch bottles or in jars, but they can't spell actual names, because they are pictographic, not alphabetic. They can be inscribed on candles, which are then burned, and either released to the wind or combined with salt, depending on the spell. Adaptable, understandable, easy to interpret, and visually appealing, Witch runes are enjoyed and appreciated by modern witches for their many applications.

# SYMBOLISM, CORRESPONDENCES, AND ASSOCIATIONS

The pictographic symbols of Witch runes are representative: Their meaning is connected to their appearance. The Eye looks like an eye, and the Rings are interlocking rings. This built-in visual parity where meaning is connected to symbol removes a layer of secrecy, which can later be reinstated by their use. An observer may recognize the form of the Wave rune, but they will not understand the context in which it is being used, so the witch may practice in safety without revealing the nature of their intention or work. Furthermore, the Witch runes correspond nicely to such genres of magickal workings as:

- **Celestial:** The Sun, the Moon, and the Star.

- **Elemental:** Flight (air), the Wave (water), Harvest (earth), and Romance (fire).

- **Polarity:** Many, but not all, traditions of witchcraft employ some sort of duality or sexual polarity in their mythology or lore.

- **Protection:** The Eye is used as a ward in many traditions. It is a talisman that protects its bearer. It is often seen in jewelry, over doorways, in cars, or in the home.

- **Fate:** The Scythe, the Crossroads, and the Rings are all associated with the hand of fate. These runes factor heavily in predictive magick.

---

### Polarity in Witchcraft

This relationship between opposites can be seen in the Goddess/Consort duality of Wicca or the gendered deities of Heathenry. It is important to note than even a masculine deity such as Odin has been depicted as an adept in feminine arts of sorcery, so the modern practitioner of witchcraft should be aware that gendered polarity is not a prerequisite to practicing witchcraft. Witch runes such as Man and Woman exhibit this concept of gendered duality.

---

# DIVINING AND INTERPRETING WITCH RUNES

## *Psychometric Divination with Witch Runes*

One way to use Witch runes for divination is through pendulum work. Use a mat on the floor or a low table for your divination work. Arrange all thirteen of your Witch runes in a circle 6 inches in diameter, starting with the Sun in the twelve o'clock position and then placing them according to your instinct.

Hold your pendulum so that it hovers above the center point of the circle, which is empty. Ground and center your energy and establish a connection to your tools, the runes and the pendulum. Come to a place of stillness and let the pendulum come to a rest. Ask the pendulum to show you "yes." When you get a clear indication of decisive movement, remember it, and then invite the pendulum to come to a place of stillness again. Then ask it to show you "not yes." At this point you should be perceiving oscillations or rotations of the pendulum depending on which movement indicates a positive response and which indicates a negative response.

After you have established "yes" and "not yes," you can begin divining with the Witch runes. Ask your questions or formulate your intention and direct these thoughts to the pendulum. You should also speak them aloud to create vibrational energy in the surrounding environment. Then, one by one, move the runestones from the outer circle to directly under the pendulum and allow the tool time to respond. See toward which runes it gravitates. Then, you may ask if the influence or outcome will be positive or negative by coming to a place of stillness while probing further. Try not to move your arm, so that the pendulum hovers above the indicated rune in a "rest" position.

For example, if you are thinking about a relationship, you can try moving Romance, then Rings, and then Scythe to get insight as to whether or not persisting in the relationship or ending the relationship might be more favorable. You may find that the pendulum is indicating toward the Scythe. Move the pendulum so that it is directly over the Scythe and ask your question with more clarity. Your first question need not be a direct question. You can simply refer to the situation, such as "my relationship" or "this class" or "my family" or "this job." Once you get an indication of the nature of the situation, then you can get an affirmation or a warning.

## Holding Space

Another method of divination with Witch runes is to sit on the floor and gather all thirteen runes into your hands. Focus on the information you wish to obtain, but do not ask a direct question just yet. Think of divining with Witch runes as the beginning to a conversation.

Focus on the situation. This means that instead of asking a direct question, such as "Does [NAME] feel the same way about me as I do about them?" visualize the interaction and say, "The situation or issue is my relationship." Repeat the issue or situation out loud three times in general terms, such as "My relationship with [NAME]," while gently shaking the runes in your hands. Your hands should be slightly cupped as though in prayer, except with your palms not touching but with pressure on your fingertips to create space. You are essentially creating a small vessel with your hands, making space but also contact. By literally "holding space" you are cultivating an energy field surrounding an opening where magick can enter. Feel the energy as you press your fingertips together, and with your last recitation of the desired insight, take a deep breath and exhale deliberately onto your runes as though you are blowing on them with a slow, sustained, well-directed exhalation; then gently drop them.

Gaze at them and identify the runes that are turned faceup and take note of the order in which you noticed them. Which rune called to your eye first? This is the dominant rune that is speaking to your situation. Pay close attention to the rune that has fallen the farthest away from you. This is your guide rune, the one that will indicate your next steps. Look for runes that are touching each other, which signifies a relationship between the message that each rune bears. For example:

- The Scythe touching Flight indicates that an ending is coming quickly.
- The Eye touching the Wave means that forgiveness and healing are possible.
- The Star touching Woman or Man represents an inspirational person.
- The Sun touching Man or Woman indicates a family member.

Take the attributes of each individual rune, note their proximity and placement, and then create a mental synthesis of their combined associations, and you will become a competent Witch runes reader. You may then progress with the conversation and ask the runes what you should be focusing on next and see what your intuition tells you. It is important to cultivate stillness along with the ability to not just ask, but also to listen.

# SPELLS WITH WITCH RUNES

Two of the benefits of using Witch runes are their beauty and simplicity. Of all the rune systems explored in this book, they are the most straightforward and do not require extensive study. This makes them accessible and useful. Some of the primary uses for Witch runes are in spells. Spells can be done for a variety of reasons in order to affect an outcome. Witch runes also work well incorporated into charms. Here are some spells you can do using Witch runes.

# Manifesting Spell

———— ❧ ————

A manifesting spell involves something you can achieve, experience, or desire. It is first imagined and then brought down into the earthly plane. A manifesting spell can be for something like a new opportunity to present itself or a new relationship to come into being.

## You Will Need

- Pencil and paper
- Yellow votive candle in a glass jar

## Directions

1. Draw the Sun rune on a piece of paper. On the other side of the paper, write down the specific circumstance that you wish to call into being.

2. Place the rune with your intention under the yellow jar candle with the Sun facing up and your intention on the bottom.

3. Allow the candle to burn down uninterrupted. Immediately after the candle has burned out, retrieve the paper, fold it, and keep it with you either in a pocket, card holder, or wallet.

4. Touch the paper and feel that it has been enlivened by sun and by fire. Allow the Sun rune to transmute your intention into reality. Think of how life depends on the sun. The sun allows things to grow. When your desire has manifested, you can burn the paper and return the ashes to the earth.

# *Releasing Spell*

———— ❧ ————

Releasing is the opposite of manifesting. It is the purging or letting go of things that no longer serve your needs and purposes. Releasing is powerful, because in releasing, you make room for new things to manifest. Thus, a releasing spell can come before a manifesting spell. For a releasing spell, choose Flight.

## You Will Need
- Pencil and paper
- Small rock or stone
- Small cauldron

## Directions

1. Draw the rune on a piece of paper and whisper to it what you most need to release.

2. Wrap the paper around the small rock or stone and place it on your altar.

3. Hold your hands over the bundle and chant your desire, spoken in rhyme:

> MOON ABOVE,
> EARTH BENEATH,
> BRING ME BALANCE.
> BRING ME PEACE.
> WHAT NO LONGER SERVES,
> THIS I RELEASE.
> TO THE WINDS,
> THE ASHES BLOW.
> AND I TAKE FLIGHT
> TO SOAR, TO GROW.

4. After you have recited this, take the rock wrapped with the rune and burn the charm in the small cauldron.

5. Allow the cauldron to cool completely and then retrieve the rock. Wash the carbon and scorch marks away from the rock under running water.

6. Carry the cauldron outside, bring the rock, and stand with the wind behind you. Pour the ashes into your hand and blow them into the air, aligned with the direction that the wind is traveling.

7. Dust off your hands and prepare for new and good things to come into your life. Accept that releasing can be messy business. Leave the rock behind.

# *Healing Spell*

_____ ❧ _____

Whether you wish to address a relationship rift or mend a grievance between two partners, choose an appropriate rune for each party. This could be Man or Woman if they have binary gender identity, or another rune (such as the Sun, Moon, or Star) that aligns closely with them. The most important thing is that your intention is clear.

## You Will Need
- Pencil and paper
- Green candle

## Directions

1. Draw the two runes, one on each side of the paper, and place the paper under the green candle. Light the candle.

2. As the candle burns down, think about what is necessary for healing to take place. It might be a physical change or restoration. The situation may require an apology or a certain gesture.

3. If a physical healing is needed, choose the Sun rune and an additional rune to represent the person. The green candle represents vitality and growth. It is also a symbol of love, as green is associated with the heart chakra. Keep the person in need of healing in your thoughts as you project your intention by focusing on the candle flame. Think of healing light entering the person and envision your intention traveling down the wick and charging the Sun rune.

4. If your intention is to heal a relationship between two people, you will need to modify the runes by selecting the rune that most closely represents the nature of the relationship. You would still use the green candle and a rune to represent the person with whom you want to heal. If it is a marital relationship, choose the Rings. For a romantic relationship, chose Romance. For friendship, use the Star.

5. The rune now becomes a healing talisman. It can be carried on the person, given to the person afflicted in order to enhance their energy and lift their spirits, or shared with the person with whom you wish to make amends.

# Banishing Spell

––––––– ❧ –––––––

A stronger dismissal, banishing is like releasing while slamming the door shut. If releasing is deleting, then banishing is blocking. For banishing, use the Scythe rune.

## You Will Need

- Pencil
- 2" × 2" piece of paper
- Black candle
- Dark, earthy incense, such as frankincense
- Small cauldron
- Pinch of sea salt

## Directions

1. Draw the Scythe rune on the paper and place it under the black candle.

2. Light the candle and also burn the incense as you envision a complete detachment.

3. When the candle burns down, burn the rune in your cauldron.

4. Once the paper has completely burned, add a bit of sea salt and mix it with the ash. Then take the black salt and throw it into a moving body of water by standing with the water behind you and throwing the salt with your right hand over your left shoulder.

5. Walk away and do not look back.

# Cord-Cutting Jar Spell

———— ✑ ————

Sometimes you need a clean break from a situation. This is where the Scythe rune can be very useful. The Scythe can be used in many ways. You can use it to remove unwanted situations from your sphere of influence or to cut down things that you no longer wish to grow. Think of how a scythe is used in life: It clears a path by removing obstacles so that you can walk on it safely. It is used for harvest—in cutting down old growth, new room is made for things to continue to grow. If you are bound to a person or situation that is no longer serving you, a cord-cutting spell using the Scythe rune can provide much-needed clarity so that you can move on from the undesirable relationship.

## You Will Need

- Pen with black ink
- 3" × 5" piece of cardstock
- 1 yard of red cord or ribbon (e.g., red satin cord, thick embroidery floss, or thin ribbon)
- Scissors
- Clean, small glass jar
- 1 black tumbled gemstone (e.g., a smooth onyx or an obsidian stone)
- 1 cinnamon stick
- 1 sprig of rosemary
- Sealing wax

## Directions

1. Draw the Scythe rune on the cardstock in black ink and place it on your altar.

2. Focus on the Scythe as you run the cord through your hands.

3. Holding the cord in your left hand, pull it from between your thumb and first finger with your right hand. As you pull the cord, you are infusing it with the intention of the person or environment from which you wish to separate.

4. Pull the cord as many times as you need. As you pull, speak aloud the following charm:

> I USE THE SCYTHE
> FOR ALL THINGS DIE.
> PROTECTED BY
> MY PSYCHIC EYE,
> THE PLAN I MADE
> NOW MUST FADE.
> RETURN TO EARTH,
> AWAIT REBIRTH.
> THE SACRED RUNE,
> THE BLESSED MOON.
> ALL THINGS I SEE
> AND BLESSED BE.
> THE MIGHTY SCYTHE
> BEFORE MY EYES.
> ALL THINGS DIE
> BEFORE THEY RISE.

5. When you are satisfied that you have projected all due energy into the cord, wind it around the cardstock bearing the Scythe rune. "All due energy" means that you have been honest with yourself, that you have been truthful and specific in your intention, that you have accepted responsibility for whatever, if any, part you had in feeding the situation and allowing it to grow, and that you are truly ready to release it.

6. Now you have a talisman of the Witch's rune bearing the Scythe with a cord wrapped around it. Using scissors, cut through the cord so that it is in many pieces. Once the cord is cut, even if you wanted to, you cannot repair it. If you attempted to tie all the cut pieces together so that they were rejoined, the cord would never be the same as it was before. This is desirable, because change is constant; it is one thing you can always anticipate. You may need to remind yourself that it is okay to let go and that it is only through these acts of releasing that we create room for the desirable relationships and situations that are manifested with the aid of skillful magick.

7. Gather the cord pieces together and put them in the small glass jar.

8. Add black stone, cinnamon, and rosemary. The color of the stone is important: Black absorbs, so any remaining energy from the severed cord is symbolically returned to the earth. The cinnamon is an offering to the spirits to aid you in your work, and the rosemary is so that you never forget the lesson or that the spell is permanent.

9. When all the ingredients are in the jar, roll up or fold the Scythe rune facedown so it fits in the jar and covers the other ingredients. Place the lid on the jar tightly and seal it shut with sealing wax.

Now you have a few choices. You can leave the jar in the vicinity of the person or environment of the broken bond, but you must act in accord. This means that after placing the jar, you will not return to this place. Whether the spell jar is discovered or not is no longer your concern because the cord is cut and the situation or relationship no longer exists. It has been transformed by magick. If you do not act in accord with your own intention, you will weaken your magick abilities. There is no rune that will substitute for acting in accord.

Your other option is to complete the transformation by returning the jar to the earth by burying it and then planting a magickal herb such as basil, mint, or catnip on top of it. This method of transformation is more involved but also effective because you will no longer see the remnants of the severed cord. Instead, you will see something that brings happiness growing in its place.

# Binding Jar Spell

Sometimes it is necessary to take magickal action in order to stop something from occurring. Performing a binding spell can be a form of protective magick. A binding spell is not to bind something or someone to you. Binding spells are to prohibit or interfere with a situation that is likely to manifest but that needs to be redressed because it poses a threat or could be a catalyst for an undesirable chain of events. For a binding spell, you can use the Crossroads rune.

## You Will Need

- Pencil and paper
- 1 foot of embroidery thread
- Clean glass jar
- Rock

## Directions

1. Draw the rune on paper and make a point in the center of the Crossroads. The point represents the name of the person or the type of action that you wish to thwart, interrupt, or stall.

2. Fold the paper, with the rune on the inside of the fold, until it is as small as it can get. As you fold, you can speak the charm:

> OUT OF SIGHT,
> OUT OF MIND,
> OUT OF TIME,
> THIS I BIND.
> WORD TO DEED,
> WITH ALL DUE SPEED,
> I HOLD THE KEYS,
> AND THIS I FREEZE.

3. Wrap a length of embroidery thread tightly around the folded Crossroads rune in different directions, leaving a tail of thread with which to tie off. When you get to the end of the thread or when the folded rune is completely covered, tie the two ends of the thread together tightly.

4. Drop the bound rune in the jar and put the rock on top of it. Fill half the jar with water and place it in the back of your freezer. Leave it there for as long as it takes the spell to manifest, usually at least a full lunar cycle.

5. On the dark moon, which is the new moon phase, you can remove the jar and bury it in a place from which it will not be retrieved.

# Handfasting Spell

_____ ❧ _____

If you wish to make a commitment to a loving relationship for the span of a year and a day, the Rings rune can be used to symbolize this meaningful and important bond of love between witches.

## You Will Need

- Scribe
- 2 taper or pillar candles
- Compass

## Directions

1. To add power to a handfasting ritual, scribe or carve the Rings rune onto the taper or pillar candles. The candles can be prepared days in advance if a formal ritual is to be enacted. The color of the candles should reflect the nature of the relationship:

    - **Red** if the primary bond is passion
    - **Blue** if the primary bond is loyalty
    - **Yellow** if the primary bond is intellect
    - **White** if the primary bond is purity

2. Place the candles on your altar with intention. Use a compass so you know which direction is north, south, east, and west. Think about yourself and your partner and place the candles on opposite sides of your altar where they make the most sense. Are you grounded and your partner more emotional? Place yours in the north (which corresponds to earth) and your partner's in the west (which corresponds to water and is considered to be the seat of emotions). Is your partner passionate, while you are content to feed that passion but may not always initiate it? Your partner's candle would then go in the south (which corresponds to fire) and yours would go in the east (which represents air, the fuel of fire). Whichever placement makes the most sense to you is the one you should choose. Maybe the two of you are passionate and grounded, or lighthearted and emotional. Or perhaps there are more than two people involved in the relationship—if so, use the

number of candles that best represents those involved. No matter what your relationship dynamic may be, choose with intention and your spell will be enhanced.

3. Each night, light the candles and move them a little closer to each other until they eventually meet in the middle. This represents your common ground.

4. On the day of the handfasting, move the candles so they are leaning into each other. This can be done by holding the candles in an inverted fashion and allowing a small pool of wax to accumulate. Then heat the bottom sides of the candles to soften the bottoms and keep the wax drippings liquid. Set the candles into the warm wax at approximately a 10-degree angle. Hold them in place until the wax solidifies. The flames of the candles will combine and burn brighter, and the two candles will appear to be partaking in a kiss.

5. Allow the united candles to burn down together. Gather any wax drippings and save them for one year and a day. At the end of that time, you and your partner can decide if you wish to continue the bond. If you wish to end the commitment, discard the wax. If you wish to remain together, melt the wax in a double boiler and pour it, along with a few drops of an essential oil that is pleasing to you or arouses you, into a new candle.

# Hexing Spell

Hexing is controversial, but it can also be very empowering and healing. When someone has truly wronged a witch—and this does happen—the witch is entitled to return the negative energy by reflecting it back to the source. You can engage in anonymous hexing, which does not directly attack a named individual but instead dissipates and deflects the residual energy of the injury away from you and back to its source point.

## You Will Need

- The Eye, Flight, and the Scythe runes, painted on stones
- Shallow dish, such as a 6" plate
- Dried rosemary leaves
- Pushpin, needle, or tack
- Black candle

## Directions

1. Assemble your ingredients on your altar. Place the three runes in a triangle pattern on the plate with the Eye at the apex, the Scythe on the side mirroring your dominant side, and Flight opposite the Scythe.

2. Scatter the rosemary along the center of the dish.

3. Using the pushpin, needle, or tack, scribe the word "hex" on the black candle.

4. Light the candle and drip some of the wax onto the center of the plate. Fix the candle on the melted wax so that it stands alone. The Eye will serve as your protection. Flight will send your intention to its target. Scythe will sever the flight path so that any negative energy will not return to you, and even if it did, the Eye would ward it off.

5. Allow the candle to burn down and then discard the remains.

# RUNES OF HONORIUS: THE THEBAN ALPHABET

While the precise origins of the Runes of Honorius, also known as the Theban alphabet, remain unclear, their use dates back to the medieval period. Believed to have been invented by Honorius of Thebes, they made their first appearance in Book Three of *Three Books of Occult Philosophy* by Heinrich Cornelius Agrippa. This work was a substantial contribution to philosophical magickal discourse, and Agrippa's influence extended far beyond his lifetime during the age of the Renaissance. Magick and religion were considered inextricably linked. Agrippa sought to grapple with the magico-religious issues of his time, issues with which we still engage today.

## Feminism

Heinrich Cornelius Agrippa's *Declamation on the Nobility and Preeminence of the Female Sex*, originally published in 1529, is nothing short of revolutionary when one considers it was written in the midst of a patriarchal society. Persistent belief in the inferiority of women was deeply ingrained in politics, philosophy, and religion, and Agrippa, a noted feminist, was an important alternate voice to the pervading misogyny.

Of all the linguistic alphabetic rune systems presented, next to the Norse runes, the Theban alphabet is probably the most widely used by modern witches. Unmistakable Indo-European influences can be seen in the graceful curves and complex patterns, which are a sharp contrast to the rudimentary staves and hash marks of earlier rune systems. Part of the enduring popularity of the Theban runes is that they provide an elegant method of expression for preserving the tradition of secrecy in witchcraft. Popular in grimoires, Theban runes are a beautiful system of inscription for labeling, consecrating, creating, and recording spells and charms; recording memories; and dedicating objects for special use.

# The Theban Runes

| Modern English Equivalent | Runes of Honorius |
|:---:|:---:|
| A | |
| B | |
| C | |
| D | |
| E | |

| Modern English Equivalent | Runes of Honorius |
|:---:|:---:|
| F | |
| G | |
| H | |
| I | |
| J | |
| K | |

| Modern English Equivalent | Runes of Honorius |
|:---:|:---:|
| L | |
| M | |
| N | |
| O | |
| P | |
| Q | |

| Modern English Equivalent | Runes of Honorius |
|:---:|:---:|
| R | |
| S | |
| T | |
| U | |
| V | |
| W | |

| Modern English Equivalent | Runes of Honorius |
|:---:|:---:|
| X | |
| Y | |
| Z | |

*Chapter 4*

# THE OGHAM RUNES OF THE CELTS

There is perhaps no tradition more steeped in mystery than that of the Druids, who were a Celtic religious class of priests and mystics. They had a profound reverence for nature and an attunement with both masculine and feminine aspects of deity, and they used henges (large circles) made of wood or stone, early alphabets, and calendars, but the Druids did not make much use of the written word. They left no manuscripts to explore. Instead, they passed down their traditions, ethos, and rituals orally, and since there are no surviving Druids today, the modern practice of Druidry is largely a reconstruction. This does not make it any less authentic, nor does it invalidate an ancient or modern practice.

Like language, oracles and tradition are in a constant state of flux and refinement. Modern witches speak their mother tongue, while literacy comes much later. An oral tradition, like a written tradition, evolves over time. The fact that modern speakers of English do not use the spelling and diction of Chaucer or Shakespeare does not lessen the importance of their own version of language; nor is the work of Chaucer or Shakespeare lessened by the fact that certain language structures and features of diction are no longer popular.

To say that a modern work is inferior to that of the past because of its modernity is to do both the present and the past an injustice. In the case of Druidism, we benefit from enlivening an ancient practice through modern interpretation, provided it is done with respect and deference to the culture of origin.

Ogham is an Irish script. It has survived because it was hewn into stone, and it was hewn into stone because it was important. While Druids were not known for written scripts, it has been theorized that they used the Ogham runes as a method of secretly communicating through gestures.

## THE HISTORY OF THE OGHAM RUNES

It is believed by some that the Ogham runic system was used solely for either divination or for ciphers; however, there are many competing theories surrounding the origin of the Ogham runes. Several theories suggest the Ogham runes came into existence after the fall of the Tower of Babel, a biblical explanation for linguistic diversity. According to the Bible, people originally spoke a single language. They began building a tower that would reach Heaven, thus encroaching upon the domain of God. In order to redress this act of human hubris, God destroyed the tower and rendered its builders unable to understand one another. In this way, the multiplicity of languages was born.

The Ogham runes bear similarities to early alphabets such as Elder Futhark and Latin. Some scholars suggest that early Irish Christians were seeking a way to conceal military and political communications from rivals who were able to read only Latin. Others see the Ogham runes as a symbol of Irish distinctiveness.

According to scholar and poet Robert Graves, who was born in 1895 and is still widely read today, all the characters in the Ogham script have a phonetic equivalent; however, some scholars claim that Ogham was a written language and was not spoken. This seems somewhat counterintuitive to what is currently understood about Druidic practices, since their mysteries were primarily maintained by an oral tradition. Since there are sounds expressed by this primitive Celtic alphabet, it can also function as language, allowing the modern witch to hear the voices of a distant age. Furthermore, each letter is named for a different tree, and each particular species of tree is imbued with its own occult significance.

The runes of the Ogham script appear as a series of hash marks, or tallies, etched along horizontal fields called "fews." The fews, also referred to as "feda," are grouped into families called "aicme." Each of the four aicme contains a series of five letters united by a common motif. The Ogham runes are read vertically along the stave, beginning from the bottom.

Even more intriguing is their dual function as a calendar; this is a powerful reminder that this method of divination is meant to transcend time, for time and its continual unfolding is central to this runic system. Thirteen months are associated with the Ogham fews, each one aligning with a specific tree.

Adding to the mystery of the Ogham runes, Graves suggested that Druids may have used the fews to communicate via a series of gestures in which parts of the hand corresponded to letters of the alphabet—an esoteric occult sign language. The four aicme, together with their five feda, can be mathematically connected to the five fingers of the hand and four points of contact along each finger. The fingertips, together with the first, second, and third articulated segments of each finger, represent the four families, while the five digits correspond to the five feda.

### Book of Ballymote

Examples of Ogham script, which is believed to date back to the fourth century, appear on tombstones and in manuscripts such as the *Book of Ballymote*. Most surviving examples of early Ogham runes are either the names of people on marked graves or indications of possession, such as land ownership. A common inscription begins with the implied phrase "stone of" followed by a specific name, followed by "son of" and a family reference, then followed by a tribal reference.

The *Book of Ballymote* includes the Ogham runes along horizontal lines, just as Graves does, while early stone carvings reveal the runes carved along the vertical staves. Orientation of the Ogham runes appears connected to the material upon which they are inscribed, and it is entirely likely that the orientation of the runes is purely practical. Whether they were first used to conceal secrets or as an instrument of sorcery, one thing is certain: Fascination with Ogham runes as an emblem of distinctly Irish culture has remained strong. These cipher-like symbols are used by the modern witch for a variety of purposes, including divining, celebrating love, welcoming newborns, celebrating family, and announcing property ownership.

# DRUIDIC AND CELTIC PRACTICES

Reverence for nature, particularly trees, and the veneration of fire are hallmarks of Druidic and Celtic ritual. Many people assume the Wheel of the Year, used by modern witches to mark the change of the seasons, was based on ancient Celtic tradition, but there is actually very little evidence to support this. The Wheel of the Year is a modern construct used by modern witches, and while it does incorporate some Celtic fire festivals, it is not authentically ancient. Its modernity does not detract from its importance. Irish monoliths such as Knowth and Newgrange indicate that ancient Celts knew about and observed solstices and equinoxes, and modern Druids continue to gather and make pilgrimages to Stonehenge on the summer solstice. The Ogham runes are found on paper, wood, and stone and were used to indicate grave markers, place names, and property ownership. Each corresponding letter represents a tree and each tree has a specific symbolic significance.

| Number | Corresponding Latin letter | Name | Meaning |
|--------|---------------------------|-------|---------|
| 1 | B | Beth | Birch |
| 2 | L | Luis | Rowan |
| 3 | F | Fearn | Alder |
| 4 | S | Saille | Willow |
| 5 | N | Nion | Ash |
| 6 | H | Uath | Hawthorn |
| 7 | D | Duir | Oak |
| 8 | T | Tinne | Holly |

| Number | Corresponding Latin letter | Name | Meaning |
|--------|----------------------------|------|---------|
| 9 | C | Coll | Hazel |
| 10 | K | Quert | Apple |
| 11 | M | Muin | Vine |
| 12 | G | Gort | Ivy |
| 13 | NG | Ngeadal | Reed or broom |
| 14 | ST or Z | Pethboc | Dwarf elder |
| 15 | R | Ruis | Elder |
| 16 | A | Ailm | Silver fir |
| 17 | O | Onn | Furze |
| 18 | U | Ur | Heather |
| 19 | E | Eadha | White poplar |
| 20 | I | Idho | Yew |

In addition to these phonemes, the Ogham runes also contain morphemes, which are combined sounds.

| Sound | Rune |
|-------|------|
| NG | |
| EA | |
| OI and TH | |

| Sound | Rune |
|:---:|:---:|
| *UI* | |
| *IA* | |

# CONNECTION TO NATURE

Ogham runes implore us to connect with nature and with the wisdom of trees. Trees are some of the oldest living organisms on earth. In trees, many lessons are to be learned. Trees embody the Wheel of the Year. They instruct us on the importance of turning inward during the cold winter period of dormancy in order to conserve energy for the full-flowering, prolific eruptions of springtime. Trees transform the energy of the sun into an energy source for growth, leafing out in the fullness of summer. Finally, trees demonstrate the necessity of letting go, releasing their leaves to blanket the forest floor and provide protection and nutrients for the next generation. Trees communicate with each other through the network of their roots. They recognize their offspring and push nutrients to their families. Their spirits inhabit the oracle, and the Ogham runes are the best conduit for this powerful aspect of nature. Here are the significant tree associations of the Ogham runes.

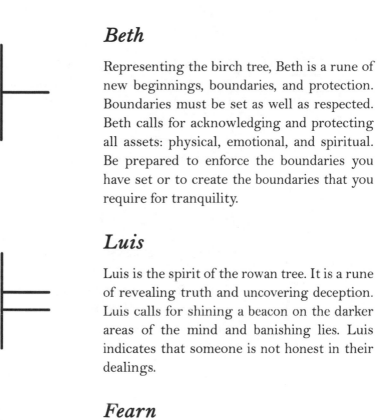

## Beth

Representing the birch tree, Beth is a rune of new beginnings, boundaries, and protection. Boundaries must be set as well as respected. Beth calls for acknowledging and protecting all assets: physical, emotional, and spiritual. Be prepared to enforce the boundaries you have set or to create the boundaries that you require for tranquility.

## Luis

Luis is the spirit of the rowan tree. It is a rune of revealing truth and uncovering deception. Luis calls for shining a beacon on the darker areas of the mind and banishing lies. Luis indicates that someone is not honest in their dealings.

## Fearn

Symbolic of the alder tree, Fearn is the rune of warriors and heroes. Fearn speaks to challenges met and obstacles overcome. Fearn encourages inner strength and fortitude, confidence, and personal agency. Fearn is a harbinger of the appropriate time to speak up, take action, and move past difficulties.

## Saille

Saille represents the willow tree and symbolizes death. This could also mean a significant closing of a life chapter, one that will not be reopened. It is a final ending of a path that will not be revisited in this lifetime.

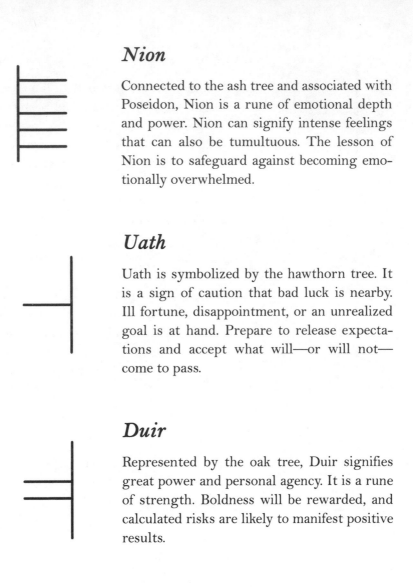

## Nion

Connected to the ash tree and associated with Poseidon, Nion is a rune of emotional depth and power. Nion can signify intense feelings that can also be tumultuous. The lesson of Nion is to safeguard against becoming emotionally overwhelmed.

## Uath

Uath is symbolized by the hawthorn tree. It is a sign of caution that bad luck is nearby. Ill fortune, disappointment, or an unrealized goal is at hand. Prepare to release expectations and accept what will—or will not—come to pass.

## Duir

Represented by the oak tree, Duir signifies great power and personal agency. It is a rune of strength. Boldness will be rewarded, and calculated risks are likely to manifest positive results.

## Tinne

Tinne is associated with the holly tree and symbolizes immortality, regeneration, and the triumph of the eternal spirit. Tinne is a rune of rebirth, new beginnings, and starting over. It may also signify a family reconciliation.

## Coll

The hazel tree is the tree of Coll. Representing wisdom, Coll is both pithy and succinct. Coll encourages direct communication with confidence. The thoughtfully written email or timely text will be well received, and negotiations look favorable.

## Quert

Associated with the apple tree, Quert represents love, fulfillment, and wisdom. Apples encompass relationships and growth, particularly partnerships where there is a strong attraction.

## Muin

Muin is a passionate rune signifying joy and exhilaration but is mirrored by a darker side in which things can get out of hand. Associated with the fruited vine, Muin can signify great heights in which the temptation is to throw caution to the wind. Poor judgment, rash decisions, or decisions made without due diligence are the lessons of Muin.

## Gort

Gort is symbolized by the flowering ivy vine representing resurrection and rebirth. Gort is the rune of beginning anew while keeping the lessons of the past. It is the emergence after difficulty, inspiration after a fallow period. It is a favorable omen that new endeavors will be successful.

## Ngeadal

With connections to reed and broom, Ngeadal is a rune of hidden mysteries and for clearing away. Ngeadal calls upon you to be both flexible and resilient, able to release and let go. Call upon your strength and be ready to move and adapt to changes when you draw this rune.

## Pethboc

A rune of sovereign power and associated with dwarf elder, which bears fruit with healing properties, Pethboc is a rune of completion. This can symbolize a promotion or graduation or a gain in social status. Pethboc heralds a necessary ending, but one that will lead to greater stability and wholeness.

## Ruis

Associated with healing, Ruis corresponds to the elder tree, which has a long association with witches. The healing may come in physical or emotional form, but it will be transformational and complete. Ruis may represent an encounter with a person who is a healer, or the healing may come from within.

## Ailm

Associated with the silver fir, which is often used as a yuletide tree, Ailm is a rune of new beginnings. It signifies growth, a fresh start, or a departure from old ways. Ailm can also represent clearing away of old patterns and releasing the past.

## Onn

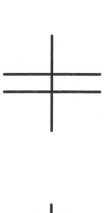

Represented by the gorse shrub, also known as furze, Onn is a rune of setting plans and allowing them time to manifest. Drawing Onn may represent that some type of short-term sacrifice may be needed in order to achieve a greater success.

## Ur

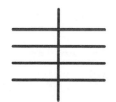

Ur is symbolized by heather. Shearing of the heather is a tradition in European and North American cultures. It represents the connection between this world and the next. Ur may be an indication that a spirit is trying to contact you. Ur is a rune of generosity and healing.

## Eadha

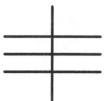

Symbolizing courage, Eadha is connected to the white poplar tree. The poplar is somewhat delicate, and drawing Eadha may indicate vulnerability. Eadha is a sign to gather strength in order to overcome what lies ahead.

## Idho

Idho of the yew tree is a rune of longevity. With regard to a situation, it is a culmination of a long journey that could signify a significant transformation and possibly even a change of identity or death. Culminations are not the same as endings, because the message of Idho is one of endurance and continuance.

# CASTING WITH OGHAM RUNES

As with any system of divination, before casting with Ogham runes, it is important to understand what you're undertaking. Communication with an oracle demands knowledge of the system and a clear purpose. Take time to set your purpose, your inquiry, or your reason for consulting the runes. Remember that the Ogham runes were a Druidic tree oracle; modern rune sets are often made of wood with the rune staves carved onto sticks. Spirits of the trees have been elements of mythology across many cultures and are not limited to Druidic reconstruction.

In addition to being a tree alphabet, the Ogham script was also a calendar; therefore, it can be quite useful for divination. Excluding the five vowel sounds, the Ogham runes construct a thirteen-month cycle, which indicates it may have been connected to lunation.

When using the Ogham runes, it is recommended that you attune not only with the phase of the moon, but also with awareness of the mythological energy of the dryad and the Green Man as well as the unending spiral of time.

Dryads are female tree spirits, often depicted as a woman's body morphed with the trunk, branches, and leaves of a tree. The dryad is a mythological being comprising feminine and arboreal traits. The Green Man is a spiritual archetype of the natural world most often depicted as the face of a man made out of oak leaves. These two archetypes are emblematic of the power of trees, and together they serve as a point of entry that personifies the wisdom of trees and can make the idea of a tree oracle accessible to the modern mind. Spiritual archetypes can also help establish context. This means that the oracle can be consulted outside in nature in the presence of trees.

Keep in mind that in addition to being connected to trees, the Ogham runes are also connected to time, and consequently, timing. This means that if you want information on beginnings or new endeavors, cast your runes during the waxing and full moon. If you need guidance about obtaining closure or endings of relationships, jobs, or situations, use the Ogham runes during the waning or new moon. The appropriate environment and the right phase of the moon will enhance your connection to the oracle because you will be thinking about not only your own queries and desires but also the characteristics inherent in the system itself.

Consult the Ogham runes when you need to know when an event is likely to occur. You may also use Ogham runes to reveal or illuminate an event from the past. Energies that are bound to time no matter the direction, be it forward into the future or far away in the distant past, can be divined with the Ogham runes. A simple three-rune spread for divination can include the season, the duration, and the resolution.

# THREE-RUNE SPREAD

When consulting the Ogham runes, it is important to first contemplate the nature of oracles. Oracles are able to traverse the bridge between the physical world and the metaphysical world through a conduit. The connection among the runes, the rune caster, and the oracle is that conduit. Any one of these components on their own is insufficient to create a channel or connection. Just as the spirit may animate and enliven the corporeal form, so too may the runes transmit the energy and information disseminated by the oracle. It is the responsibility of the modern witch to honor these ancient traditions with respect and understanding.

Beginning by acknowledging and integrating the nature of time, especially the Ogham aspect of calendar, you can divine information using a simple three-rune spread that focuses on a particular season and the duration of a situation or event, and forecast in which future season the issue will resolve. Draw the runes at random by mixing them up and choosing three without looking. The order in which you draw them will reveal three things: when or how the situation began, how long it will last, and when it will resolve. To simplify, you can think of the first rune as the energy of the past, the second as the present, and the third as the future.

### Season
Working with the Ogham runes is preferably done out of doors in the presence of trees. Perhaps you are able to see runes naturally expressed through the growth of bough and limb. Take a moment

to bring about a calm and clear state of mind, then draw the first rune. This first rune will reveal the seasonal point on the Wheel of the Year in which the event or interaction first occurred. For more influences, you may consult the phase of the moon or astrological influences during that time.

If the event or interaction is known to you, this is an easy way to "test" your prophesying ability or to establish either the connection or lack thereof with the oracle. If your answer does not resonate because it is inaccurate or completely wrong, you need to make some adjustment. It is possible that the oracle is asking you to observe from a different point of view, just as a leaf on a tree experiences life as part of a whole that it never gets to see. Take such an indication as a call to refine your question and see if there is something else you are being called to look at. If the time of year of the inception of the event does not fit, you may need to investigate the zodiac sign of the particular month and see if the oracle is calling out a particular relationship in the past that may be informing your present situation. For example, if you are inquiring about the status of a relationship and you know that the relationship began in March, but the rune of season drawn is Eadha, which rules the autumn equinox, this could indicate a significant person born under the sign of Virgo. The more you engage with the oracle, the more familiar you will become with how and what it communicates.

## Duration

Duration includes the length of time that the effects of the event or interaction are felt. This could manifest as consequences, effects, or other elements such as memory. Duration also includes the amount of time you have to take action and prepare for the next phase. Duration is in relation to the initial occurrence.

## Resolution

The resolution will reveal the time of year when the next energetic shift is due through the tying up of loose ends, a cycle of completion, or a transmutation of energy. Chapters end and cords are cut and new experiences will come into being. This rune position will indicate when this will occur.

# CALENDAR MONTHS ASSOCIATED WITH THE OGHAM RUNES

Use this table of correspondences to assist in interpreting the three-rune spread with Ogham runes. Since the Druidic calendar does not follow the Gregorian calendar, a modern interpretation will require some adjustments, because the runes Ailm, Onn, Ur, Eadha, and Idho represent specific turning points such as the solstices and equinoxes. Ailm and Idho are connected to the winter solstice, Onn with the spring equinox, Ur with the summer solstice, and Eadha with the autumn equinox. Those turning points are points of change and represent elevated power and have increased importance.

| Month | Tree |
|---|---|
| December 24–January 20 | Birch |
| January 21–February 17 | Rowan |
| February 18–March 17 | Ash |
| March 18–April 14 | Alder |
| April 15–May 12 | Willow |
| May 13–June 9 | Hawthorn |
| June 10–July 7 | Oak |
| July 8–August 4 | Holly |
| August 5–September 1 | Hazel |
| September 2–September 29 | Vine |
| September 30–October 27 | Ivy |
| October 28–November 24 | Dwarf elder |
| November 25–December 23 | Elder |

# FIVE-RUNE SPREAD

For a more in-depth reading into a circumstance or to uncover the nature of a situation or event, you may choose to use a five-rune spread. The five-rune spread follows a vertical line, giving it a natural visual attunement to the Ogham runes themselves. While Ogham runes appear in both horizontal and vertical orientations, vertical is the more frequently occurring of the two. The first rune you draw represents the self, and it goes in the middle. The following runes are drawn and placed from bottom to top as follows:

- **Position one:** Bottom far below center. This rune represents the distant past. It could also indicate a past life or someone from a previous incarnation.

- **Position two:** Directly below center. This rune is the recent past, the influences surrounding the events that are just behind you.

- **Position three (already drawn):** Center. Your present situation or state of mind, revealing how you are doing in this moment.

- **Position four:** Directly above center. This rune is your near future and represents the influences that are about to occur or will occur within the calendar year.

- **Position five:** Far above center. This is a more distant future and will give you information about the effects or consequences that you will experience beyond the present year, based on the information currently at hand.

# TEN-RUNE SPREAD

The ten-rune spread is modeled after the star motifs that were popular during the Middle Ages in the British Isles. If you are using Ogham sticks, the spread will make a star shape. If your runes are on tiles or stones, it will look like a center point surrounded by a circle. Draw the runes without looking and then place them in the following order according to how they were chosen:

- **Position one:** Center. The first rune you draw represents yourself in the present moment.

- **Position two:** Crosses the center. The second rune is your obstacle. This is the lesson or the challenge that you must overcome.

- **Position three:** Above center. The third rune represents your highest hopes and the best possible outcome. This rune is a reflection of your desire.

- **Position four:** Below center. This is the action that you will either take or be subjected to. It is the energy that will lead you to the outcome.

- **Position five:** Right of center. This rune will indicate the disposition of those around you and how they relate to your question. Family, community, and connections are revealed here.

- **Position six:** Left of center. This represents your inner emotions. This rune will illuminate your internal state of balance or lack thereof.

- **Position seven:** Northeast, between positions three and five. This rune represents your weakness; an area that you must address.

- **Position eight:** Southeast, between positions four and five. This rune will indicate your outward appearance—how you are seen by others and what kind of energy is in your surrounding outside environment.

- **Position nine:** Southwest, between positions four and six. This rune is your rune of strength.

- **Position ten:** Northwest, between positions six and three. This rune represents your future and the influences that will manifest with your present course of action.

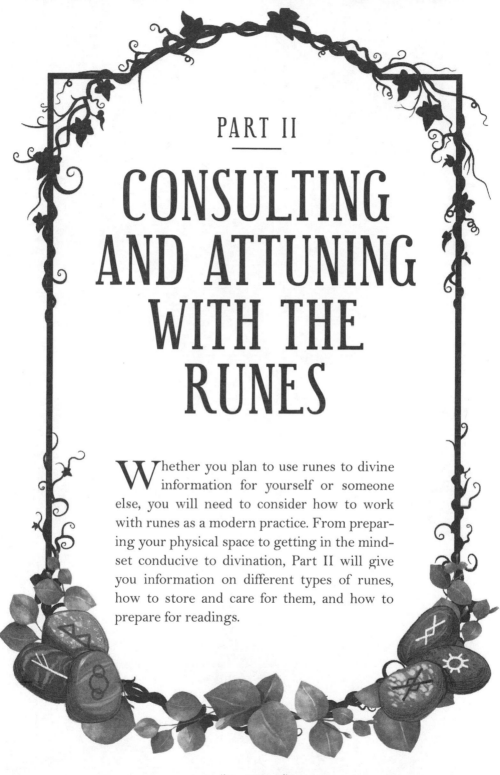

# PART II

## CONSULTING AND ATTUNING WITH THE RUNES

Whether you plan to use runes to divine information for yourself or someone else, you will need to consider how to work with runes as a modern practice. From preparing your physical space to getting in the mindset conducive to divination, Part II will give you information on different types of runes, how to store and care for them, and how to prepare for readings.

## Chapter 5

# CHOOSING THE RIGHT RUNIC SYSTEM FOR YOU

Now that you've explored several different systems of runes, you must make a choice of which system is most appropriate and authentic to you. You may find that you resonate with one system and stick with that one for a long time, or you may want to learn different systems and use them for different purposes. This choice is informed by many criteria. You may want simply to engage with the oracle most closely connected to your own ancestral line. If you don't have details about your ancestral line, your choice will be different, as not everyone has the access to family histories.

The history of humanity is one of exploration, growth, achievement, and innovation but also of monstrous cruelties, exploitation, and conquest. To delve into this takes an abundance of strength, as the oracle demands honesty and openness and a willingness to examine the less savory parts of our collective past decisions and actions. This is not to say that runes are exclusively bound to the past; they are not. Oracles are fluid constructs that transcend time. Runes are systems that are by nature fluid and changing. As a conduit of oracular wisdom, runes are as significant now as they were when they first made themselves useful and widely known.

# EXPLORING YOUR ANCESTRAL ROOTS

Ancestry is an extremely difficult topic with which to engage. Migration, assimilation, and even the abduction of people can make the study of lineage daunting. At its best, genealogy is revealing, and at its worst, it is emotionally devastating and woefully incomplete.

It comes as no surprise that many people feel disconnected from their ancestral lines. Family stories are often incomplete or inaccurate, and in many cases, it is difficult if not impossible for a person to fill in the blanks in order to get a picture of where they belong in the grand scheme of things. The rise in popularity of DNA test kits is a testament to the longing for ancestral information that many people feel.

Engaging with the distant past can reveal generational trauma, and while confronting a difficult family history can be challenging, it can also open pathways to healing. Tracing a family line can help you understand your current path and lead you to a runic system to which you may already be connected. It may also reveal a system you may want to avoid. Alternately, since the widespread use of runic writing died out in the Middle Ages, reclaiming a system on your own terms can be very empowering. Reclaiming can give you a stronger sense of self, a connection to your ancestral line, and an understanding of the geographical migrations that brought you to your present life.

Your predecessors made choices that ultimately led to your incarnation in this time in this place. For those seeking esoteric knowledge or for those whose family history was lost, choosing a new means of expression such as runes can fill those voids. Since runes are connected to language, understanding how we refer to one another and the origins of the words we use can impact how we interact with the oracle.

For example, it is widely understood that indigenous Americans almost always had a name for themselves that meant some variation of the word "people"; however, the tribal names by which they became known (and consequently by which they are historically described) were most often the descriptors given by their enemies. For this reason, there are tribes who do not accept or acknowledge the names given to them by their enemies. An example is the so-called Sioux tribe, more correctly distinguished as Nakota, Lakota, or Dakota, depending on the particular dialect spoken by this indigenous American tribe. They were the original inhabitants of what is now known as Minnesota, but they did not refer to themselves as "Sioux." The tribe bears the name of a reduced form of the word *Nadowessioux*, which is a pejorative term. This name was used by the Ojibwa to describe them in a negative manner. Because the term means "little snakes" and is alternately interpreted as "enemy," it is highly unlikely that members of this tribe chose to refer to themselves as such.

Reclaiming fraught language could be seen as an act of defiance or even empowerment as is evidenced in modern times when historically oppressed People of Color have embraced and reclaimed language that was once meant to demean and insult them. The same is true of the word "witch." For many, it still conjures up negative images of ugly and dangerous women; however, for those who have reclaimed and embraced the word, it conjures up images of beauty and power, and of strength and confidence. This powerful reclaiming can also be applied to runes. You should choose a runic system with knowledge and intent. A combination of self-knowledge and historical knowledge will allow for a stronger oracular connection because you choose from a place of knowing before engaging with the mystery.

# A STARTING PLACE

Begin where you are. The choices or circumstances of your elders have led you to the place where you are today, and the land upon which you walk is an integral part of you. Explore the language and traditions of your place and time. If family records are lost or if your history is unknown to you, connect to your present. There is much to be learned about where you are now, and it is equally as valid as where you came from. If you are occupying stolen land—and unless you're a member of an indigenous people, that's the case—acknowledge it. If choice was denied to your ancestors, make a choice to be here now and embrace the present moment with all the challenges, pain, and potential that holds for you. If your roots run deep, connect with them by honoring all the steps along the path that have brought you to this present moment. Appreciating the journey, however fraught it may have been, can bring you to a more grounded and centered state that will be the basis from which you can experience occult energies. Without a strong sense of self and purpose, it is easy to get swept away when delving into oracles. Self-awareness, open-mindedness, and balance are key.

## Connecting with the Land

Start by acknowledging the connections that you already have, the ones that are well known to you. Explore the history of your birthplace and be open to feeling uncomfortable. Delving into history is akin to delving into darkness. There are shadows and skeletons to confront. Do not shy away and overlook truth. Orient yourself as a sentient, compassionate, and empathetic being. You may begin to uncover mysteries and connections just by understanding where you are.

Think about the migrations of your own lifetime. While some people may live in the same place and set down deep roots in a family home for generations, in modern life it is equally, if not more, common to change locations. Your own patterns of change may reveal connections to certain runic systems. Frequent moves align more closely in an energetic sense with Norse runes because the Nordic people were well known to be explorers. Ogham runes may resonate more with a person who has been more stationary, as the Ogham runes are deeply connected to trees, which require established roots. The Witch runes are going to work well for those who revel in esoteric and occult practices, for these are the most modern and least documented, and, consequently, more receptive to the associations we place upon them.

### The Vegvísir

One example of runic reconstruction is the popularity of the Vegvísir symbol. An eight-rayed rune, the Vegvísir has been seen emblazoned on everything from jewelry and clothing to skin in the form of tattoos. Heavily associated with Vikings, the Vegvísir most likely originated from the British Isles and made its way to Iceland. The Vegvísir does appear in the *Huld* manuscript, which was compiled from several Icelandic grimoires around 1860 by Geir Vigfússon. There is some question as to whether the Vegvísir is truly of ancient Norse origin. Although runes were used in Scandinavia before they were used elsewhere, it is difficult to imagine that something as important to a culture as the Vegvísir would go unrecorded for hundreds of years by the people who supposedly invented it.

Star motifs were more widespread in the British Isles than they were in the more northern regions; however, the Vegvísir was not recorded until the 1800s. Since then, it has taken root in the collective consciousness of humanity as a Viking symbol of protection and guidance, particularly from and through dangerous weather and storms. With the devastating effects of climate change visible on all continents, from raging wildfires to rising sea levels, it is easy to understand how and why the importance of the Vegvísir will continue to grow as this powerful symbol becomes adopted by practitioners of different types of magick.

# CENSUS DATA

Surnames and census data can yield information about how long a family line has been connected to a certain area. This information is public and easily searched, but it is important to know what to search for. Interrupted family lines due to adoption or changes of surnames can make the task daunting, but interviewing living family members and investigating records that align with known names and places is a good place to start. Take a few surnames from your research and try writing them out in a rune system. Acknowledge the form and see how it affects you. Is it pleasing to the eye? Does it make sense to your soul?

Early uses of runes included naming objects and showing ownership of items. Use the tables in Part I to create a personalized rune stave with a family surname and see which calls to you. You may also choose to do this experiment using your magickal name. Say or write a surname or magickal name that you want to start with.

Then choose a system such as Norse, Ogham, or Theban and do the following:

- If you are using Norse runes, draw a horizontal stave and find the phonetic equivalents of the name you wish to write and then scribe the characters from right to left along the horizontal stave.
- If you are using Ogham runes, draw a vertical stave and scribe the runes from bottom to top.
- If you are using Theban runes, you can directly transcribe.
- If you are using Witch runes, select the runes that you find most personally poignant.

In magick it is necessary to hone your instincts because you must rely on them. In order for your intuition and inner voice to become strong, they must be used frequently. This means engaging with your ideas and feelings, refraining from judging yourself, and becoming unattached to outcomes. If you want to see something specific, there is no need to consult an oracle because you are not open to new information.

Not every magick practitioner resonates with or has a connection to their family of origin. It is customary for spiritual witches to choose a magickal name for themselves that is known only to fellow coven members. For secular witches, using a surname or a given name or even the names chosen to identify oneself on social media are the more appropriate choices, because in naming yourself, you reclaim personal power. Whether you wish to explore a connection to an ancestral name, a magickal name, or another name by which you are known, try writing your name from right to left in runes and see what calls to you. This is a highly personal way to determine which rune set is the best choice for you.

# DNA TESTING

While not 100 percent accurate, DNA tests compare your sample with known haplogroups of people who share similar DNA. In the absence of family records, a DNA test can reveal very general locations and patterns of migration going back several generations. You can then compare results with any family stories of which you are already aware. This may give some insight into where you can trace your geographical origins. Again, this is for the purpose of self-discovery and not to suggest that you're prohibited from using some type of rune system due to ancestry; however, if you should discover a conflict, it is best to be aware before delving into occult systems.

Runes were present during tumultuous parts of human history, times of not only cultural exchange but also domination. If you originate from a culture that was assimilated by a more dominant culture, then a system of language and divination from that dominant culture might not feel authentic to your practice. Choose with knowledge and intention and let wisdom and intuition be your guides.

# CULTURAL ASSOCIATIONS OF DIFFERENT RUNIC SYSTEMS

Another factor that will influence which runic system you should use for divination is understanding some of the lingering cultural associations that shape our understanding of both ancient and modern civilizations. For example, Norse cultural associations are strongly connected to earth, fire, and water. Volcanic activity and eruptions factor into Norse mythology and history, often as descriptions of a battle. Viking explorers were also known for mastering the arts of sailing. If your zodiac sign is an earth, fire, or water sign, you may be attracted to Norse runes along these types of correspondences and connections:

- Earth as a mutable, powerful, life-giving entity
- Fire as an instrument of creation and transformation
- Water as a symbol of distant travel, overcoming obstacles, and victory

Ogham runes were used by the Druids. Druids are known for a deep reverence for the earth, an oral tradition for passing on magick, and even more notably for human sacrifice. Part of Druidic practice was to build a Wicker Man, often from willow boughs, and create an effigy inside of which a sacrificial victim was burned. This practice was an allegory for the death and rebirth of the God.

Rituals of death and rebirth persist even in Christian traditions, which ironically have a historical aversion to witchcraft. Considering that congregants still gather on Sundays to acknowledge the death and rebirth of Jesus symbolized through the ritual of Communion, where the body and blood of Christ are represented in bread and wine, perhaps the pre-Christian traditions do not seem as strange.

The same themes pervade modern observances and are widely accepted, although they involve symbolic sacrifice instead of actual sacrifice, such as the Catholic practice of giving something up for Lent or the pagan ritual of burning a Yule log. Consequently, more humane and modern associations can be drawn from Druidic culture to include acknowledgment of the cyclical nature of life and that death is not something to be feared. Rather, it is a rite of passage that connects us to universal consciousness and is an inescapable part of the human experience. Ogham runes may be the correct choice if you are a fire, an earth, or an air sign who resonates with these associations:

- Fire as a potent symbol of purification, destruction, or transformation and change
- Earth as a constant source of inspiration and devotion
- Air as an active symbol of rapid change or growth

The Witch runes will appeal to practitioners who are visually oriented. A nonalphabetic, symbolic system will be easier to use for some people, and there are fewer runes in that system, so they can be learned quickly. While the Witch runes can't be used to express a magickal name, they can be incorporated in magick in other ways, such as use as individual talismans, in psychometry, and for fortune-telling. People who have some psychic ability and want to become more adept with symbols will be drawn to the Witch runes.

# RECLAIM YOUR POWER AS A WITCH

Runes bring the past alive while bringing power to the present. Reclaiming runes as part of a magickal practice is a valid exercise for any witch. A witch bows to no one and creates a magickal reality based on experience. There is no right or wrong way to experience magick. Some traditions are of the initiatory path and require commitment, discipline, and scholarship, while others embrace a spiritual practice unconstrained by dogma. Still others gravitate toward the image of witch as a powerful icon and do not experience their personal brand of magick as a connection to a spiritual path.

Using runes is an aspect of reclaiming because they are ancient and are not in wide use as they once were. Interest in runes is experiencing a resurgence in much the same way that witchcraft is inspiring a new generation even though it is not a new practice. There was a time when witches were feared, persecuted, hanged, and burned. Some say this is because their power was a perceived threat. Others say witches were persecuted for their looks, their healing ability or its inverse, or any number of nonconforming activities or appearances. Using runes is a way to connect with the power of the witch, as divination has been a staple among occult practices for thousands of years. From the earliest astronomers of Babylon to the rune-masters of the Middle Ages, looking elsewhere and beyond for answers is central to the practice of magick.

### Declare Your Power

The first step in reclaiming power is acknowledging that you have it. Even if you have chosen an initiatory path, initiation done by a high priestess or priest does not directly confer initiation because the initiation is done by the Gods. The officiant acknowledges and honors the work that the initiate has done and the initiate's connection to the divine. The transformation and act of declaring a path or dedicating to a deity or even a lifestyle is first always personal. The outward trappings are emblems of this internal transformation. No one may truly say when a witch has awakened. Only you know that for certain. A shift in consciousness can happen spontaneously or after years of diligent pursuit. Acknowledge yourself as a creator of magick, and you are ready for step two!

### Own Your Power

The next step after declaring your power is owning it. This means being true to yourself and operating as an ethical and evolving learner of occult skills, such as rune casting. It means that you tap into your own sources of power by attuning with phases of the moon and making sure you set aside time for mindfulness to increase your awareness and receptive abilities. It means being honest about your developing psychic acumen, finding your strengths, and exploring them. You may discover that you are an empath, meaning you are able to feel what others are feeling. Or perhaps you are clairvoyant, able to sense and understand unspoken or hidden information. Whatever your abilities are, embrace them and share your gifts.

## Use Your Power

Once you have declared and owned your power, it is time to use it. The concept of power is multifaceted, but if you approach it as an expression of your highest aspiration for yourself and for the good of all, you will never confuse "empowerment" with "power over another person."

In seeking personal autonomy, this same consideration needs to be extended and applied to all beings so that your work does not take on a destructive power. This is not to say that magick cannot be used during times of darkness or strife, but creating chaos should not be the goal. (There are enough disasters in the world without witches adding to the imbalances of the elements and the environments!) For example, if you are a fire sign, adept with using fire in magick, and want to celebrate the ancient Celtic fire festivals with bonfires, please consider all safety precautions. In dry climates, an ember and a breeze can be disastrous. Using your power means understanding its strength in the physical as well as the metaphysical world and moving accordingly for the benefit of all beings.

---

### The New Burning Times

During the peak years of the witch hunts, which occurred in the late 1500s and lasted until the mid-1600s in Europe and until the late 1600s in the United States, you did not have to be an actual witch to be tried and executed as one. As your understanding of the diverse nature of humanity grows, so too should your acceptance of "otherness." You cannot call yourself a witch while failing to acknowledge the modern equivalences of people put to death or denied their humanity based on their actions or appearance.

---

# Calling Back Your Heart

——— ✍ ———

Engaging with runes can stir up strong, conflicting, and confusing emotions. People don't normally turn to oracles when life events are status quo. Life is tumultuous and chaotic, a churning cauldron of molten metal and fire in a vessel of solid but shifting rock. This is an inescapable fact, and we move accordingly. It can be easy to get lost on the path. Self-doubt, mistakes, and regrets can force us to confront things we would rather not examine, but runes can help. By giving voice to a *galdr*, a magick song in which runes are sung, and manipulating sonic energy vibrations, the magick practitioner can call back forgotten sources of strength. Yes, the earth is tumultuous and chaotic, but it is in these conditions that beauty is forged. Create your *galdr* by first distilling your desire or need into a single word and then transliterating that word into its phonetic rune equivalents and then singing it out loud. Write the word, and then write the word in runes. To create your own *galdr*, pronounce the runes as you improvise a song using your own voice.

## You Will Need
- Index card
- Pencil

## Directions

1. Take a simple word such as "mind," "heart," or "body" and write it down on an index card with a pencil.

2. On the other side, create a transliteration in runes. Consult the phonetic equivalences and speak your word aloud, and recite the name of each rune you used to create the transliteration. The word should reflect whichever aspect of your life is in need of attention or healing. For example, if isolation and anxiety are disrupting you, focus on "mind." If isolation has brought you feelings of alienation, loneliness, and hopelessness, choose "heart." If your health is not what it should be, choose "body." Use the following charm:

[WORD]
[GALDR]

I CALL YOU BACK TO ME.
I CALL BACK MY [WORD].
[GALDR] IS MINE.

3. Repeat this as a mantra or a chant, using the card to help you alternately focus on either the character, the word, or the pronunciation.

4. Allow yourself to experience the return of your natural and balanced state so that you may go forth from a place of love, health, and confidence.

# DIFFERENT ENERGETIC PROPERTIES

Reclaiming and calling back your power are the first steps before engaging with different types of energetic properties. Once you know yourself and understand your receptive abilities, such as how well you can remember and recall what different runes represent, you are then ready to interpret things that are more difficult to perceive. Energetic properties are subtle. They inhabit both the substance that runes are carved on as well as the symbols inscribed on the substance. Think of the elemental properties of witchcraft and how much variety and diversity of meaning they can represent. When working with air, the practitioner may engage with any number of energetic properties from gentle breezes that welcome in new growth to the more formidable winds of change that sweep through dramatically and leave transformation or even destruction in their wake.

Fire has significant energetic properties as well. There is the candle flame that illuminates the darkness, and there are raging wildfires that reduce substances to their purest form. Again, we see the propensity for change, either through redirection, transformation, or destruction. Water energy can be harnessed as a light spring rain that nourishes and cleanses, but it also represents deep, unknowable mysteries as well as complex emotions. And the mighty earth is both life-giver and repository for generations, civilizations, and ancestral lines, eventually absorbing and reclaiming all growth, all life, as it returns to source energy. The blessed earth brings forth all, sustains all, and also absorbs all in death. Because you are seeking out the runes and the mysteries they reveal, you will need a strong foundation in interpreting subtle energies.

Divining information through an oracle is subtle. You will have to make connections. Yes, runes have names and definitions and meaning, but they also have spiritual energy, and the more sensitive you allow yourself to become, the more accurate your rune interpretations will be. Rune casting requires studying but also touching and turning and choosing and placing. You can decide to become a free diver and read all you want about swimming and snorkeling, but until you jump in and feel that cold water and the pressure of the depths and your own personal limits of how long you can hold your breath, you will not really have an understanding of what the task requires. Discipline yourself to listen for things you cannot hear, to reach for things beyond your grasp. Engage your senses and open yourself to receiving and make your rune practice active.

The first law of thermodynamics reminds us that energy is neither created nor destroyed; however, it can be transformed from one form to another. The second law of thermodynamics illustrates this transfer of energy: If something cold comes into contact with something hot, the result is the hot object becomes colder and the cold object becomes hotter.

### Runes and Divination

Engaging with runes as a method of divination aligns with the first two laws of thermodynamics. The physical object on which the rune is graved will retain some of the metaphysical energy transferred to it by the person who made it as well as the meaning of the symbol inscribed on it. And when consulting an oracle, there is an exchange of energy between the petitioner or questioner and the source point. Some witches identify the source point as the Goddess or God. Other witches may engage with the energetic principle of the spirit of an ancestor. Secular witches may identify elemental energetic confluences as the source point, while some will point to their subconscious, believing the answers to questions and affirmations emanate from a deeply personal source or power from within.

The law of inertia states that an object in motion will stay in motion and an object at rest will stay at rest until it is acted upon by an outside force. Your magick is that outside force. It is the fundamental power to set things into motion or halt them completely. The more you cultivate your own awareness of these principles, the easier it gets to interact with them and manipulate and affect them. Regardless of your personal beliefs, in modern witchcraft, there are energetic properties attached to all oracles, such as runes. Runes are relevant, immediate, and tangible, and can be used by anyone with an elevated psychic or spiritual awareness as well as people just starting to seek out and develop those abilities.

When you work with runes, it is important to establish a successful connection to the oracle; therefore, before you form your query or frame your situation, and well before you ever attempt to read for another person, examine the energetic properties with which you are comfortable engaging, and then move accordingly.

Oracles are free from the constraints of our human understanding. They endure across time, space, and geography. You determine your entry point to the oracle. Modern witchcraft is pure reconstruction because so much of traditional as well as ancient practice is completely undocumented and inaccessible except on an intuitive and metaphysical level. It is not possible to travel back in time and observe ancient Druidic practice to see firsthand if a specific deity was invoked before Ogham runes were carved on a surface; therefore, it is essential for the modern oracular reconstructionist to clearly define these energetic principles for themselves, depending on what type of witchcraft they practice.

# ENERGETIC PRINCIPLES

For rune work, we'll delineate energetic principles in three ways: spiritual energy, external energy, and internal energy. Choose the one that is most appropriate to your craft and build from there. Identifying an energetic source point is essential to establishing a clear connection. While there is no right or wrong way to practice witchcraft, consulting an oracle such as runes is a distinct occult endeavor, and it should be done in a certain way. Consulting an oracle is a form of communication, and runes are linguistic and symbolic systems of communication.

You wouldn't initiate a phone call or an email or text without having at least some idea of whom you wish to engage or what outcome you'd expect. The same is true of working with runes. If you wouldn't call upon someone you didn't trust for guidance and advice, then do not consult the runes if you have not established a connection. If you are having difficulty defining the energetic properties with which you wish to work, the following sections will help. Just as when you are calling customer service or ordering something, you may not intimately know the person or organization with whom you are engaging, but you'll acknowledge certain rules.

## Spiritual Energy

If you are a spiritual witch following an initiatory path, it is likely that there is already a strong connection to the deities in your practice. Working with runes will add another layer onto your tradition because, in addition to maintaining a connection to the deity, you are now also seeking communication.

This communication may function in much the same way as any other devotional ritual. You can make invocations and establish a channel. In spiritual witchcraft, it is customary to make formal invocations to the directions, the elements, and the deity or deities with whom you've chosen to work or to whom you've devoted your spiritual path. Depending on the type of devotional or initiatory path—and these paths are numerous—the method of invocation should follow the tradition that you've chosen.

There are instances when you'll feel guided or pulled to a particular deity. This is a sign of a strong connection. You can dedicate a set of runes as a formal pathworking (using them in a ritual fashion during heightened energetic times, such as auspicious planetary alignments or full and new moons) in order to maintain connection to source energy in the form of reverence for your chosen deity; however, it is also common for the deity to choose the practitioner. Some important things to consider are the deities who were honored and worshipped at the inception of the runes. Exploring the pantheon of Norse, Celtic, and Greek deities and seeing which ones resonate with you is a valuable exercise.

## External Energy

Runes are often used in religious practices, but they do not have to be. Many practitioners of modern witchcraft do not consider themselves to be practicing a religion. This does not lessen the validity of their practice. Witchcraft is not inherently dogmatic and does not have centralized leadership. Nor is witchcraft restricted to a particular belief system or ethos. Witchcraft can take on many forms. For some witches, it is closely tied to knowledge of healing plants, reverence for natural spaces, or awareness of planetary alignments and astronomical events. Witchcraft manifests in recipes, family traditions, stories, and crafts, and it is centered in the home, in the kitchen, or at the hearth or hedge. Some witches even identify with one specific element and declare themselves "water witches" and the like. Runes can be used in witchcraft without formal invocations to Goddesses or Gods. But the modern witch would do well to examine and explore where they think the energy of the runes is coming from.

For witches whose practice and traditions are centered on wellness, weather, elements, and environment, establishing a connection to rune work is based on elemental and ancestral energy. Witches attune themselves to their surroundings, knowing which guests to welcome and which to dissuade from entering; this same principle applies to runes. A nonreligious witch, or a person who considers themselves on a path of secular witchcraft and has a different religious allegiance to another denomination, such as Christianity or Buddhism, may establish and maintain a deep connection to the oracle by incorporating runes into their practice. Some witches consider witchcraft a cultural expression of things they eat, herbs they grow, and crafts they make while they still maintain other religious allegiances. This also means that, for example, a hedge witch, whose focus is on esoteric knowledge and mystical interactions within the spaces described as "between the worlds," is no more or no less qualified for rune work than the green witch, who possesses a strong affinity with healing plants and an alignment with nature as a steward of the earth. Both can create or dedicate a set of runes to eternal wisdom, strength, resilience, and growth as manifested in the beauty and power of the earth. A kitchen witch can use runes to define or declare ownership of important tools, acknowledging the connection between runes and fire.

*Part II: Consulting and Attuning with the Runes*

Fire festivals were central to Druidic practice, and volcanoes influenced Norse mythology. While not much is written about the volcanic activity that Viking explorers encountered when they arrived in Iceland from Scandinavia, they clearly accepted that natural phenomena were accepted as a part of life and not heavily associated with religion. *The Poetic Edda* does contain a reference to Loki's awakening and to the fire giant Surtr, which coincides with the volcanic eruptions that took place in the first millennium. However, Norse mythology does not contain rich or effusive lore that connects this type of natural occurrence with an expression of religion, as do other cultures where volcanic activity is more common (for example, the South Pacific). Instead of the formal invocation done with reverence as described in the recommendations for working with runes as a part of a spiritual practice, the witch who chooses runes can use them in the presence of representations of elemental powers. These representations are the "tools" of witchcraft. For example, a lighted candle, a cup of water, and a dish of salt that are kept near the runes will help establish a link between the natural magick of the elements and the witch who wishes to establish a line of communication through these powers.

## Internal Energy

A secular witch who has little interest in initiatory traditions and relies on their own intuition and instinct may still use runes as an effective means of connection with the oracle.

Oracles do not require any sort of belief in order for them to exist; they work no matter the experience or type of path the diviner uses. Rune casting is no different from any other endeavor in that some witches will have a natural aptitude and ability, while others will have to hone theirs or need to rely more on interpretations. Those with a talent for linguistics, an aptitude for symbol and pattern recognition, and a love of study will have more success faster, but this does not preclude any type of witch, secular or spiritual, from effective rune casting.

In the absence of a deity, an elemental, or another external focus, the secular witch is going to be forced to levels of self-examination and awareness that might be quite uncomfortable at first.

If, as a solitary witch, you have a strong connection to family, you may want to engage with the oracle as though you were speaking to an ancestor, a confidant, or a trusted elder. If you do not have a sense of this connection, you may want to first engage in a meditative practice to empty your mind of mundane thought and open yourself to a channel of heightened awareness of your own intuition. In order to trust your instincts and intuition, you must first become acutely aware of them. Objectivity can be difficult to attain when working alone, so the solitary secular practitioner may wish to reach out to another like-minded individual in order to have some assistance either in casting or reading and interpreting a rune spread. It is a way to maintain impartiality and accountability on your path to becoming a rune-master.

Consciously choosing the energetic properties with which you wish to engage is an empowering step to becoming an adept rune-master. Although there are many variables to explore, the end result is impressive. Learning a rune system increases your knowledge of ancient cultures. Establishing a connection to the oracle enhances your ability to communicate on a psychic level. Understanding what is involved in a rune cast and how to read runes elevates your magickal skill set.

There will always be people who use runes for entertainment, for curiosity, or even to make money by casting professionally for others. While there is nothing inherently wrong with curiosity and entertainment, runes are complex and deserve a depth of study. The more time and interest you invest, the more insight you will receive and your abilities to predict and interpret will grow. Developing your magickal skills will make you a more powerful witch no matter which method of practice with which you engage.

# PATHWAYS AND CHOICE

Choosing a pathway and beginning to work with runes is a thrilling and fascinating endeavor. It gives you access to an ancient mystery, an oracle that has transcended time, locations, and cultures. Modern spiritual practitioners such as Heathens, Druids, and Wiccans all use runes for divination. Heathenry and Druidism are based on the ancient cultural traditions of northern Europe, and modern devotees seek to re-create and reconstruct the rites and rituals of the past. Some modern practitioners reinvent these connections with inspiration and knowledge gained through personal gnosis.

Gnosis is considered empirical spiritual knowledge gained from personal experience and not learned from books or legends and lore. Sometimes many people will get the same messages or information through gnosis, which can be extremely validating, but this validation will not come from any published or publicly recognized source.

Wicca is a modern religion that uses iconic constructs of the past, but it is not based on reconstruction. Its spiritual paths are very different, but one thing they have in common is that they are all modern interpretations of practices drawn from the distant past. Each spiritual path has a unique rune system. However mysterious their origins, rune work and divination practice remain popular aspects of modern witchcraft. Embracing the unknown with a deliberate intent to increase psychic awareness and communication with the unseen realms is a worthy endeavor. If you do not have a spiritual tradition, you may still find yourself called to working with runes. Here are some examples of pathways of witchcraft in which runes may be used.

### As a Solitary Secular Practitioner

This type of rune work involves reading for yourself or another person for the purpose of gaining personal guidance and wisdom. You'll choose a rune system and may rely on intuition and instinct to interpret messages and meaning. The rune system is chosen by personal preference or an abstract affinity or alignment; it need not be based in anything other than how you perceive yourself or wish to be seen by others.

### As a Tradition, Craft, or Practice

Runes are used in a more ritualistic way when you incorporate oracular communication in other aspects of your craft. You can use runes alongside other nonreligious methods of gaining insight, such as psychometry, meditation, and astrology. Choose the rune system based on knowledge passed on by elders, through family ancestral origins, or by cultural affiliation through adoption or marriage. You may even have a strong preference for or affinity with a particular system.

## As Part of an Initiatory Path

Runes are conduits between the practitioner and higher spiritual powers. Runes may be incorporated into a coven activity with the spiritual practitioner becoming adept at mastering runes and using them in a ritual context, even providing rune readings as part of their offering to their spiritual community. Rune readings are less spontaneous and are done with reverence for the deity, for nature, and for the oracle itself, and this may mean that the practitioner pays special attention to the manner and method in which runes are consulted. This might involve using techniques such as grounding and centering before attempting a reading; clearing or cleansing the runes before and after each reading; and invoking powers to aid and guide the practitioner toward a deeper experience and a richer understanding about the multiple forces with which they seek to engage.

No matter which pathway to rune work you choose, runes remain accessible to all who wish to explore their inherent mysteries. The depth of your practice and how well you cultivate your connection to the oracle will be determined by your preferences, needs, aptitude, and ability. The only wrong way to use runes is as pure entertainment with disregard for their origin, historical application, and modern power.

# Chapter 6

# RUNE KEEPERS

R unes combine archaeology, anthropology, linguistics, literacy, symbolism, and divination into a fascinating study. They may inspire a passionate attachment. Accurate readings that allow you to discover new ways of understanding can lead to rune reading as a fulfilling hobby on one level and an expression of deep devotion on another. The study of runology is respected at universities across the world and has been for hundreds of years. Runes attract individuals from across the world, and they have a unifying effect, as though rune casters all share a secret yet common language.

## TYPES OF RUNE KEEPERS

Anyone who pursues the study of runes on any level gains something, whether it is a psychic connection, an appreciation for history, or the satisfaction and pleasure that comes from unraveling a mystery. There are some things to consider when you keep a set of runes or multiple sets of runes for different purposes. How you keep, use, and interact with your runes will depend heavily on your personal practice of modern witchcraft. Now you will learn more about the modern study and use of runes and the different types of scholars, enthusiasts, hobbyists, and occultists who are all connected by their knowledge of and passion for runes. For example, there are:

- Runologists (scholars)
- Runatics (hobbyists)
- Runemal (occultist practice)
- Rune-masters (occultists who not only practice but also instruct)

All these people use runes in different ways for different reasons. There is much to be learned from a wide range of rune keepers who have different attitudes toward and perspectives on the power and purpose of runes.

# KEEPERS OF SECRETS, REVEALERS OF MYSTERIES

### *Runologists*

Runologists are keepers of academic, archaeological, historical, and scholarly information about runes. They spend great amounts of time and energy deciphering lexical runes and perhaps an equal amount on distinguishing lexical runes from non-lexical runes. Lexical runes can be translated, while non-lexical runes are primarily for decoration or adornment and do not have any literal translation.

Form, purpose, and meaning are studies of runes within the context of archaeological discoveries. When a rune-bearing artifact is discovered, archaeologists and historians focus on determining the use of the object and the significance (if any) that the runic inscriptions communicate. Runes have been used on a variety of objects, such as drinking horns, jewels and brooches, everyday items such as combs, and significant monuments like grave markers. By studying the link between the objects and their runic inscriptions, runologists have determined that runes do not always translate, but they always give a glimpse into the past. Knowing that the use of runes was varied makes the modern uses of runes, such as divination and adornment, historically accurate.

Runologists were responsible for solving the mystery of the Mustang Mountain Cave runestone, which was discovered by hikers around 2012. The discovery of a defunct Baltic script in Arizona near the Mexican border sparked a flurry of speculation about twelfth-century explorers from Europe arriving in North America prior to the advent of Columbus's notable "discovery." Were the carvings there to signify a gravesite? Eventually the theory of early European settlers was debunked—the runes were carved by a nearby resident, probably in the 1990s. Debunking the Mustang Mountain Cave runes did not take long due to the fact that the author of a website featuring the now dead Sudovian rune script bore the same surname that was carved in the stone and also lived nearby. It is important to note that the ease with which runologists revealed the modern nature of the purported Sudovian runes did not stop the story from being widely shared and reported. One can only imagine the Norse God Loki enjoying this bit of trickery.

---

### Heathenry

Heathenry is a modern revival of polytheistic pre-Christian religion that focuses on traditions and customs that originated in Germanic Europe, while Ásatrú is a type of modern American Heathenry that draws its customs from northern Europe, particularly Scandinavia.

---

## *Runatics*

Those who describe themselves as "runatics" are rune hunters and seekers who delight in discovering evidence of runes. Runatics are passionate about runes in a nonreligious way but still hold them in very high regard. Even in the United States, which does not have an indigenous lore surrounding runes, people gather in their communities for celebrations centered around runes because they love them. One such example is the annual festival in Heavener, Oklahoma, where town residents and travelers gather together in spirited festivities to show their pride and affection for their local runestones and artifacts, particularly the Heavener Runestone. Discovered in 1830 and identified as rune-bearing in 1923, the Heavener Runestone is now a main attraction of a state park and boasts its own celebration featuring feasting, ax throwing, fencing, and traditional blacksmithing.

A runatic will be keenly interested in any new developments in runology, particularly if a runologist can date and validate a runatic's rune discovery or decipher a rune carving from antiquity. Runatics are hobbyists who love runes, delight in their discovery, read about them, actively seek rune sites as excited tourists as opposed to solemn pilgrims, use runes as décor, and celebrate runes through secular festivities.

## Runemal

"Runemal" is the word for the magico-religious practice of rune casting where traditions are taught to initiates by their elders as a sacred rite. Runemal is an oral tradition that may seem counterintuitive because if a tradition is oral, then there doesn't seem to be a great need for a written system such as Ogham runes. However, Druids were also known for legomonism, which means that the direct channels of knowledge are hidden. So while runes were used by Druids, the runes were not used to record their rituals or rites. These were passed down orally and remain secret. Modern runemal is mainly associated with modern Heathenry (*Runemals* and *Heathen* also happen to be the names of popular video games). While this may seem offensive or blasphemous to initiates, it is a testament to the power of runes and the importance they hold.

---

### Other Uses of Runes

In addition to the commercial gaming use of runes, runic symbols have also been adopted as political symbols. In Texas around 1980, a magickal society called the Rune-Gild was formed. This group is heavily informed by modern Heathenry, and is also described as a synthesis of the Left-Hand Path, traditionalism, and Heathenry where politically nationalist and racialist ideas (such as white people who believe the white race is superior) are incorporated into a religion (unlike Ásatrú, which is apolitical but has been known to produce racialist offshoots).

The "Left-Hand Path" refers to a practice that is evil or dark. The Right-Hand Path and the Left-Hand Path in modern occultism are diametrically opposed. The right represents the existence or importance of a moral code, while the left is defined by the taboo absence of morals. Just because someone is using runes does not mean that they are wise or benevolent. To ignore the unsavory and dangerous ways that runes have been co-opted by racists is a mistake. You must engage with runes having a thorough understanding of how symbols can be corrupted through intention, particularly when an evil intention is reinforced by a group and gains political traction. Sacred symbols can degrade into offensive emblems in a very short time, and it is unfortunate and inauthentic that runes have become associated with fascism by some. While these dangerous and commercial associations with runes exist, they do not define nor do they represent the true scope of rune casters and rune-masters.

### Rune-Masters

Rune-masters are highly skilled and knowledgeable rune casters who have trained others to become rune-masters as well. There are also self-proclaimed adept diviners who read runes on a professional level. There is overlap among many of these different rune enthusiasts, but what distinguishes a rune-master is their ability to teach.

#### Traditionalism

Traditionalism is the practice of adhering to established beliefs; it is in opposition to modern practices. A traditionalist would never partake in eclectic Wicca or espouse the syncretism found in modern New Age practices, such as the blending of Eastern and Western traditions. A modern witch might feel comfortable using runes as part of a meditation or a chakra balancing, but a traditionalist would not do that. A traditionalist stays within the conscribed behavior and customs dictated by their specific path.

# MISAPPROPRIATING RUNES

While there are more than one hundred places and objects in North America that bear runes, all of them are relatively modern, created during or after the eighteenth century. Runes themselves are not problematic. What becomes problematic is when enthusiasts use them to deceive or pervert their meaning. Furthermore, it could be considered vulgar and disrespectful for a magico-religious practice to be appropriated for video games like *Runemals, RuneScape,* or the Rune Factory series were it not for the prolific presence of non-lexical runes. If runes were used by ancient people just for decoration, then why can't they be a part of modern pop culture? Historically, runes are not *always* a language or a system of magick.

Many genuinely ancient rune artifacts defy deciphering and have no apparent translation whatsoever. This leads us to believe that the correct use of runes was entirely up to the user. It also may suggest that literacy was not as widespread as the runes themselves. If adornment and decoration were historically accurate uses, then appropriating runes for an entertainment does not seem entirely uncouth up to a point—the point being that the historical use of runes was personal, often secret, and frequently undecipherable, but not necessarily commercial.

While historical evidence suggests that runes were not used in a commercial fashion, this is not the case today. Selling sets of runes, selling rune readings as a service, and using runes to sell entertainment are altogether modern. Modern witches who are uninterested in creating personal magickal tools by hand will no doubt find commercially made runes a convenience.

## Runes for Commercial Purposes

Some modern witches will find commercial availability of runes distasteful, while others will welcome it. Some witches will gladly pay for a rune reading, while others are uncomfortable mingling the exchange of money with their magickal practice and consider it taboo. If someone has an aptitude and ability for reading runes and provides a valuable service in providing insight, access to an oracle, and information to someone who has no interest in the pursuit of dedicating themselves to learning an occult system of divination, then why should that person remain uncompensated for their expertise? The United States has laws that prohibit fortune-telling. Although they are rarely enforced, they exist to protect people against fraud and deceit. No matter your interest in runes, whether it is academic, esoteric, or commercial, interacting with runes and with others honestly is the best way to ensure that your path will not deviate into darkness and deception. There is nothing inherently wrong in buying a set of runes or paying someone to read them for you. And there is nothing wrong with charging money for performing divination for others, provided that your skill matches your price. Yes, creating your own runes and becoming an adept rune reader is a worthwhile endeavor, but over time, the runes themselves have taught us that there is no single correct way to use them.

# WHAT ARE RUNES MADE OF?

No matter which medium carries the characters of the runes, it is almost always some material inextricably linked to the earth. Runes carved on seashells or on ephemeral materials are less common, the one exception being paper, which is still made from cellulose plant material. While surviving manuscripts from antiquity featuring runes are rare, they do exist.

Runes have an air of permanence about them. They can be additive or subtractive, meaning that they can be painted onto surfaces and thereby add to the substance of the talisman, or they can be carved, where material is removed.

The magick of the runes inhabits all manner of materials from the lowly bones of wild and domestic animals to the glittering ore that inspired exploration and conquest. Runes can be carved on twigs or on jewels. Runes can even appear on dice. Sets of runes designed to be thrown by chance can fit on a single die. No matter their form, runes speak to their rune casters and creators across many levels.

## *Natural Materials*

Runes are most often made from natural organic or inorganic materials. Since it is well known that ancient runes were carved into rock, those who wish to align with ancient energy would do well to choose or create a set of runes that are carved in stone. Rock and stone are examples of natural inorganic materials used for runes. Wood, bone, and shell are organic because these organisms have had a life cycle and all contain carbon. Most rocks and minerals are inorganic because they are not carbon-bearing and have not lived. Runes are also heavily associated with trees, which makes wood another appropriate medium for runes. Wooden staves and cross-section slices of branches are examples of organic material.

Runes have been carved into antler tips, as well as bone shards and pieces from a variety of animals, including deer, sheep, and buffalo. It can be argued that using the bones of an animal for a sacred purpose is a way to honor the life and death of the creature. Those who work with animal spirits may be more comfortable attuning to a set of runes carved in bone and incorporating animal energy and reverence in their practice.

Runes were also inscribed into metal objects, including precious metals such as silver and high-karat gold. Runes have been hammered into rings and brooches and on scabbards, swords, and coins. Notable examples were the Gallehus drinking horns, discovered in the seventeenth and eighteenth centuries and made of gold. One included a runic inscription in Old Norse. Ostentatious and lavish, these artifacts were stolen in the nineteenth century, presumably for the value of the gold. Today a replica can be seen in the British Museum; it was re-created from intricate drawings of the drinking horns.

Runes are often made to appear quite beautiful. In addition to metal options, modern rune crafters offer rune sets carved into semiprecious stones with metallic staves. This opens up a whole new level of energetic endowment, because gems and crystals are widely used in magick due to the states of consciousness they produce in those who handle them and use them in magick. For example, gems and minerals are frequently used in meditation, grounding, centering, spellcraft, charms, and other magickal workings such as jar spells and talismans. Runes are also seen on ceramic tiles.

## HOW TO CARE FOR YOUR RUNES

You should care for your runes the same way you handle any other instrument of divination or magickal tool. Most likely, a modern witch would not leave their athame in the bottom of their kitchen utensil drawer, nor would their wand end up nestled at the bottom of a tote bag. Runes are magickal and should be treated as such. How you care for and handle your runes will be determined by the material from which they are made. Caring for runes made of stone means that you wrap them individually when you are not casting with them so that the surfaces of the stones do not abrade or scratch each other. Caring for runes made of wood includes keeping them well clear of your candles and oils, treating them like they are special, and not allowing dust and dirt to accumulate on them.

Consulting runes is most effectively done in a ritual. The ritual does not need to be elaborate, but as with many things, the more energy and effort you put into your practice, the more you will get out of it. Enter a state of mind that allows for expanded consciousness, engaging with the intentional desire to be receptive to messages, insight, warnings, and affirmations. How you handle your runes, the color of the cloth pouch that you wrap them in or the type of box you keep them in, and the place in your home where you store them will all have an impact on how well they work for you.

# HOW TO STORE RUNES

To have a set of runes is to manage a small collection of highly magickal objects that need care and accounting. It is very tempting to carry around a single rune for reference, remembrance, inspiration, and comfort, but then you might discover that you've misplaced the chosen rune and now have the frustrating experience of working with an incomplete set. You can store runes in a dedicated pouch, in a small box, or wrapped in a cloth. Consider the acquisition of a specific satellite pouch that you are not likely to lose track of. This will help you stay organized and keep the set together.

It may be tempting to gift a single rune to someone. Resist this temptation by thinking of your set of runes as a single entity. You do not want to lose a part of them. Successful reading requires a complete set, so it may be wise to acquire or create more than one set: a sacred set of runes dedicated for individual use and another to take on travels, one that you are less attached to and can part with more easily without disrupting your ability to consult the oracle and engage with spirit. Having more than one set allows you to engage with more spontaneity as well. There may be times when you need to do a quick "check-in" and pull a single rune with the question, "What are the energies surrounding this circumstance?"

You may also want to collect different rune systems. Once you have gained experience with a simple set of runes, such as Witch runes, you may feel inspired to learn a more esoteric system. Beginning with Witch runes could be advantageous because they are pictographic and the symbols are fairly self-explanatory, so they require less memorization. Witch runes also do not require any transliteration for their use, while creating bindrunes (runes used in combination with each other) from Norse runes does require it.

## Consider the Material

How you store your runes will be influenced by the material from which they are made. Runes carved into semiprecious stones can be quite beautiful, but if they are kept in a pouch, eventually they will get scratched and worn by rubbing against one another. If your runes are made of stone, you may wish to consider keeping them in a box where they can lie flat in a single layer. That way, they will not incur any damage. Runes that have the staves painted on them will also be subject to wearing if they encounter too much friction. Choosing a decorative box can make storing runes aesthetic and magickal.

You can store your runes facedown before drawing a rune for consultation with the oracle. If you choose a lidded box, the inside of the lid should be lined with a soft fabric. Use a removable lid in which you can cast the runes. This is a particularly useful method of casting when using the Witch runes, which are small in number and usually painted on stones (unlike Ogham runes, which are often carved or burned into sticks and require a larger working surface area for in-depth spreads).

Similar to shuffling a tarot deck, you may place the runes with the staves facing down and rearrange them until you feel satisfied that they are in their correct position for drawing. To determine the "correct" position, you must rely on your intuition and observation. The runes will often "tell" you when they are in the correct placement. You may feel a sensation that you need to stop rearranging them; a rearrangement seems to hit a snag, which makes you pause and stop. You can also rearrange them until you feel clear in your head that your question is correctly articulated. Whichever way that the runes convince you that they are ready to be read, you will then pull as many as you need for the type of spread you wish to do.

Drawstring pouches are also popular choices for storing runes. Choose one of ample size so that the runes are not stuffed in too tightly. Depending on the size of the runes and what material they are made from, a 5" × 7" pouch will suffice for most sets. You also want to be sure you can reach into the pouch easily.

### Drawing Runes Unseen

It is a frequent practice to draw runes unseen by relying on intuition. Which one is your hand drawn to? Which stone or shard or coin reaches for you? These are experiences that you may encounter when drawing runes from a pouch.

You may also decorate and personalize the pouch. Since runes were frequently used for identifying objects and even mundane applications such as labeling, you adorn a rune pouch by embroidering staves from right to left on the pouch itself. There is a power in labeling. It is more than an expression of possession and ownership; it is a type of bond. Creating a rune pouch embroidered with a transliteration of your name in runes along with a description of the contents of the pouch is a worthwhile activity. It's aesthetic and meaningful, but also cryptic, which is a huge part of the fascination that witches have with runes. It will also help you learn the runes faster.

### Interacting with Your Runes

The more interaction you have with runes, the more neural pathways you start to develop with them. The physical composition of your brain will actually change. In studying runes, you are essentially learning a language. Multilingual people have greater brain density than monolingual people. They possess more "gray matter." Learning the numerous aspects of the runes will physically change you.

Storing runes away from direct light and heat will preserve them. Direct light can lessen the vibrancy of even stone. While charging runes in the sunlight may be tempting, this is best done only on occasion. It doesn't mean you should avoid charging runes by placing them in direct sunlight, but rather you should be aware that this can eventually degrade the saturation of colored stones whether the color is natural or not.

### Runes Carved on Colored Stones

Most semiprecious stones are (or should be) marked if they are dyed or natural in color. It is always a good idea to ask because this will give you information about the ethics of the seller. A reputable seller will tell you if the stones on which your runes are carved are natural, dyed, or heat treated to enhance their color.

### *Using an Altar*

If you have a sacred space such as an altar that you use for divination work, you can arrange your runes on the surface and then cover them with a dedicated altar cloth that you can also use when you do rune readings. Covering the runes with a cloth, keeping them in a pouch, or storing them in a box shows respect for the oracle. Treat your runes as though they are valuable, and do not be too casual about consulting them. This will also help you establish balance, as information and insight can be alluring, especially when you're trying to address, resolve, or change a situation.

# PRACTICES TO CULTIVATE

To become a successful rune caster, establishing a personal practice is essential. This means a commitment to studying the origin of the type of runes with which you have chosen to work, learning their individual attributes as well as how to read different rune spreads. As a consistent practice emerges, you may find yourself able to express yourself creatively through runes, using them for divination, decoration and adornment, communication, and other appropriate uses.

You want to allow time for the information the runes give you to acclimate into your psyche. If you think a reading is incorrect, wait awhile before attempting another consultation. Think deeply about what the runes are showing you and glean what insight you can. It is possible that there are already things in motion that have not yet made themselves known. Exercise patience, discretion, and respect for the runes, and you will strengthen your attunement.

# STAVE, SYMBOL, AND SOUND

In the beginning, you may wish to familiarize yourself with one rune at a time. Focus on only one rune for a week. This can be a physical rune from your set or it can be a drawing with notes recorded in your grimoire. Even a set of characters on index cards can be a helpful tool in learning to read runes. Break down the task bit by bit. Do you want to know the names of the runes, their sounds, or what they represent? Set a priority for yourself and move on once you have accomplished your first goal.

Focusing on one rune at a time is very manageable, but there are so many different aspects of runes, so you'd be wise to determine which element you want to engage with first. For example, you could choose a single rune and study its lines and memorize its form. You could learn its name and, if you are so inclined, its pronunciation as well. Or you may want to first memorize all the names of the different runic characters, and once you are clear on the visual differences between Beth and Nion or Laguz and Ingwaz, then you can begin associating the divinatory meanings with each character.

## Runes As Alphabet

Remember that in addition to being a system of divination, runes have also served as tools of literacy. When you look at runes from many angles, you may be surprised to find that they are literally spelling things out for you. If your primary interest is in divination, you might be fine with just memorizing the associated meanings of the symbols. But if you want to use runes deeply, you will want to synthesize their many features.

Think of the phonetic and symbolic meanings of runes. Do you want to be able to pronounce them? Perhaps, if you're of Irish ancestry, you are drawn to your mother tongue and you would like to see your Irish surname written vertically along an Ogham stave.

Listen to the power of your own voice as you attempt to pronounce runes, and think of it as if you're acquiring a new language. You can even draw upon the things you already know. Do you know someone who has a corresponding initial or name that resonates with the sound that correlates with a particular rune? Creating associations that are unique to you and your understanding can accelerate your success. Essentially, you are creating new neural pathways in your mind to acquire a new symbolic language. In addition to having esoteric meanings, runes are also quite literal. Make connections in your mind among the stave, the symbol, and sound, and use mnemonic devices if they are helpful to you.

## Stave

At its most basic definition, a stave is simply a line. But upon this line you may inscribe a mystery, a secret, or a cipher. It could bear the symbols of your identity or represent a God of antiquity. Study each stave and take note of the linear and curved forms. Think of their associations. For example, a cross can represent a choice or an important decision. It can also represent an obstacle. A curve can be a smile or a bend in the road, something that is on the verge of transformation or something unexpected. A straight line can be seen as a clear path. It could represent forward movement or a complete standstill.

Understanding the multiple meanings that a stave can represent is key to interpreting runes, especially if you wish to delve into reversals or alternate meanings based on how the runes are positioned. Reversals are an entirely modern addition to traditional divination. Think of other systems, such as tarot, for example. Early tarot cards resemble playing cards and read the same no matter which way they are turned. As illustration and symbology grew, more complex meanings, such as opposites and alternates, were assigned to cards that once were represented by suits and numbers that had no up or down (much like the face cards on modern playing card decks).

If you view runes as the multidisciplinary alphabetic systems that they are, then there are no reverse meanings. Some runes are the same no matter which way you look at them; it would be impossible to tell if a reversal was drawn or not. Furthermore, linguistically, reversals make no sense. An upside-down Latin or Anglo letter does not have an alternate meaning; it still represents the same lexical and phonetic value. And Ogham runes are used horizontally as well as vertically along a stave, making it irrelevant to describe one position as "up" and another as "reversed." Furthermore, with Ogham runes, many runes are inversions of other runes. They are considered unique characters and not reversals of another character. For example, in the Ogham script, the second aicme is just the first aicme reversed, but these two families represent entirely different consonants and trees. You can spend hours trying to decipher if you drew Beth, the birch tree, or Uath, the hawthorn, because they are visual inversions of each other.

If you are drawn to reversals and wish to consider multiple associations of meanings, chances are you will not commit to learning the names of the runes backward, although backward messages have always had a place in modern occult practice because some practitioners deliberately wish to obscure information in order to preserve its secrecy. No matter in which direction they are turned, they are the same rune. If you draw a rune upside down, turn it right side up to read it. There is nothing about any alphabetic rune system that suggests alternate meanings or pronunciations because a character is upside down.

### Touching Runes

You can also learn about runes in a tactile way. Trace the pattern with your fingertips so that you know it intimately. Try writing in runes. Picture them in your mind and find your starting point. See where the journey takes you as you commit to learning each rune, stave by stave, curve by curve, and row by row. You may find inspiration and answers in the scribed lines themselves, lessening your dependence on the interpretations of others. This skill will become especially useful in later chapters where generative motifs and originality are explored.

### Symbol

Symbolism is as applicable today as it was a millennium ago. Stories, myths, legends, and lore all contributed to the world view and the cosmological understanding of the universe and each person's place in it. Understanding symbols and what they represent is an important part of any magickal practice.

Every occult society uses some sort of symbolism. Whether pictographic or linear graphic, symbols have an important place in witchcraft. Round motifs, three-way motifs, four-way motifs, quatrefoils, pentagrams, hexagrams, rayed symbols, star symbols, and planetary symbols are all widely used in witchcraft. Think of runes symbolically and allow yourself to engage in modern and personal interpretation.

Symbols are akin to doorways through which intuitive or spiritual information can travel. They can activate and enhance our understanding. Even a surface understanding and acknowledgment of what runes look like can reveal insight. For example, in the Elder Futhark Rune Row, Teiwaz bears a strong resemblance to an arrow. How does that form evolve in your mind and what insight can you gain from your own instinct? Do you start at the point where the tip of the arrow originates and draw a mental line away from it? Or is it more natural for you to move toward the apex, and how does that reflect on your current situation?

Envisioning a rune as you draw it can be quite revealing. If your instinct is to move away from it, ask yourself if there is something you are trying to avoid or shy away from. Then try reversing the process. How does it feel to envision moving toward something? It could be a goal, a physical destination, or another situation requiring swift movement. It could also be a reminder to stay focused.

Any archer knows that in order to improve, they must always stay on target. Deviating from the goal only ensures that you will never hit it. If your arrow misses the bull's-eye, do not give up and aim for the outer rings instead! Keep the form of each rune in your mind and you will establish a strong connection to each one, and eventually you will know them all by heart.

Ogham runes are a little easier to explore because each family bears similar staves and their main distinction from one another is the number and orientation of the hash marks, where some intersect the stave and others are perpendicular to the stave. You can memorize them in groups of motif and number, organizing your mind to recognize which trees and which meanings align with perpendicular staves, diagonal staves, and intersecting staves. Each rune can be seen as a tiny grove or an individual tree.

## Sound

Since runes are alphabetic and have phonetic attributes, they are pronounceable. While this may feel uncomfortable at first, speaking runes aloud creates a sound vibration that is transformational. Spells are imbued with heightened power when spoken aloud. While this does not in any way lessen the power of the written word, there is no denying that a well-crafted spell spoken in rhyme has a mystical power unlike any other.

Begin by saying the name of each rune. Think of yourself as opening up a dialogue. Speak directly to your runes, calling them by name one by one. You may find that they are speaking back to you. Once you have gotten comfortable with their names, try pronouncing their sounds. You will find the phonetic equivalents in Part I. The next step is then creating bindrunes through sound. A bindrune is a combination of two or more runes, usually along a shared stave. A bindrune can be written, and it can be pronounced. To create a bindrune, start with something simple like the initials of your first and last name. Whisper them to yourself and see how it impacts your understanding of how runes work.

Germanic, Celtic, and Italic are three of many divisions of the Indo-European languages, which belong to the most prevalent linguistic family on earth today. All of these languages are related to one another, creating a cross-cultural link among speakers of many different languages and runes. It is believed that all Indo-European languages have a common point of origin dating back five thousand years. Only the Afro-Asiatic family of languages is older.

Language is fluid and ever changing and will always be so. Adapting language is something that human beings have always done. It is not necessary to translate your runes or your intention into German, Icelandic, or Greek, for you are not attempting communication with another speaker. You are centering yourself as a manifesting witch, creating audible vibrational energy in order to deepen your connection to an oracle.

# WHAT TO AVOID

As you familiarize yourself with your runes, you may find yourself consulting them frequently. This is fine as long as you do so with an understanding of the energetic principles with which you seek to engage. The temple of Delphi, where ancient priestesses sat over a crack in the earth and inhaled vapors that emanated from the crevice as a way to channel the oracle, is said to bear the adage "Nothing in excess," and it is particularly noteworthy that this enduring phrase is so closely connected to an oracle. "Harassing" the oracle can actually make it less effective, so understanding the balance point is essential. If you find yourself consulting runes for a myriad of situations, becoming overly dependent on them, or wanting to pull different runes multiple times in one day because you are dissatisfied with their message, this may be a sign that you are obsessing and need to dial back your interaction a little bit.

## Treating Your Runes

Runes are often made from organic material such as wood and bone or inorganic material such as metal and stone. All of these materials are porous to a degree, and they will absorb not only energetic vibrations but also oil from your fingertips and oxides from the air. Sunlight, salt, water, and smoke will all impact the appearance and feel of your runes over time. If you are interested in consecrating your runes using an essential oil blend, do so with the understanding that you will permanently change their appearance.

Runes made of wood and bone are more porous than those made of metal and stone, but all are subject to eventual oxidation. Metal runes should be stored in as airtight a condition as possible. The less exposure to air, the more they will retain their finish. Oxidation occurs over time, and it is not necessarily undesirable. It appears as a dark patina, and depending on the metal, oxidation is not always difficult to remove. Anti-tarnish cloths do contain chemicals, though. You will have to consider this if you have an aversion to using anti-tarnish products on your runes.

Using an essential oil blend to dress and consecrate your runes may seem like a suitable ritual, but again, only do so with care. First of all, essential oils are volatile, meaning they are easily absorbed into the skin and you shouldn't touch them. First, you must become adept at diluting or blending oils so that you do not damage yourself. Next, you will need to determine how the rune staves are inscribed on your runes. If they are painted on, an oil can dissolve the paint and deform or erase the symbol. If the rune staves are burned or carved on, then using an oil will not affect the symbol. However, if your runes are made of wood, then the oil will discolor the wood. This is not necessarily undesirable, but it will most likely be permanent. This is due to the porous nature of wood and its ability to absorb. It is not necessary to coat your runes with any kind of lacquer or sealant. Whether they are wood, metal, or stone, they will pick up trace amounts of whatever they come into contact with, so take care to make certain they come into contact only with the things you want them to.

Salt is often used for purification of magickal objects, but it has corrosive properties. It is appropriate to clear and cleanse your runes with salt or salt water, particularly if they are newly acquired or recently handled by someone other than yourself, but do not immerse your runes in salt water for any length of time. If you feel called to use this method, remember to make it a short meditation. For example, you may wish to rinse your runes by pouring water over them instead of soaking them, or place them in a shallow dish and pour water over them, but let them steep only for about as long as it takes a joss stick to burn. Of course, if your runes are made of wood, don't submerge them at all. They will either float on top, depending on the type of wood, or they can absorb water and become warped, split, or otherwise damaged. Avoid damaging your runes and treat them as though they are valuable, because they are.

## Runes Are Personal

Think of runes as a personal item. They are dedicated to and are specific to an individual practitioner. There are some items that you simply do not lend out. This is not a sign of being closed off from one another, but more of an exercise in autonomy and establishing personal boundaries. You wouldn't lend your toothbrush or lipstick to another person, and you should not lend your runes out either. Remember they are porous and can absorb more than oils or water. They can also retain the vibrational energy of anyone who handles them. This residual connection should be yours.

Another important thing to avoid is self-doubt. Whenever you begin a new undertaking, there is always discomfort that arises from a new experience. If you feel uneasy and unsure about your ability to use runes, remember that everyone has varying levels of psychic ability and that any ability can improve with practice. The use of runes ranges from ornamental to unintelligible. You don't need to be a psychic medium or a scholar to use runes "correctly." Evidence points to the fact that many historical users of runes were barely literate, if at all. This is probably the reason why so many artifacts bearing runes are completely confounding. As long as you are using runes ethically and not to deliberately spread misinformation or cause confusion with intention, then you are using them correctly.

# Chapter 7

# RUNE CASTERS

There are many different methods by which to engage with runes. You can pull them at random or choose them with intention, throw, toss, or carefully place them. A rune cast can be methodical and deliberate. It can also be chaotic and random. The method that you choose will depend on your preference as well as the type of spread you are doing. In Chapter 5 you learned about the different spiritual energetic principles through which we filter our interactions with the oracle for divination. Familiarizing and choosing which field of influence is guiding your desire is key information that you will need to clarify for yourself before you proceed with casting.

For instance, for a single rune reading or check-in, you may wish to draw at random from your pouch or from the array in your box. The random choice is liberating if you are seeking to confront something that is beyond your control. Accepting and allowing the random chaos to unfold can lessen its importance and bring a sense of immediate peace to a situation. Letting go of outcomes and allowing yourself to relinquish control diminishes your ego and allows room for a stronger oracular connection. Conversely, if there is a situation that requires reigning in, then you will want to use a deliberate pull and a controlled spread. Neither technique has value over the other; they are dependent on the energetic principles that are present. Using the appropriate—a better word than "correct"—method will give you better results. In establishing a link to the oracle, the method of choice should be in alignment with the energies that are inherent in your reasoning for engaging with the runes in the first place. The most appropriate rune cast is the one in closest alignment to the oracle, the rune caster, and the issue or question.

# ACTIVITIES AND EXERCISES STRENGTHEN YOUR PSYCHIC ABILITIES

Divination, also known as "seeing beyond," is both a talent and a skill. Talent is inherent, as each individual has particular aptitudes. You have a strong suit or unique ability in some capacity; however, talent is not a fixed entity. It can be developed and grown. It can change over time. Talent can wax and wane, depending on how much and how often it is nurtured.

Divination is also a skill, so people who lack a strong inherent talent can develop psychic abilities through improving on the skill. As with any other discipline, occult or otherwise, in order to develop your divination skill, you must commit to a consistent level of intentionally developing your ability.

Think of any artistic or athletic pursuit. Any endeavor that requires engaging multiple functions of the brain, such as memory, empathy, or sight, can improve with repetition. Repetition on its own is not enough. If you are simply repeating mistakes, then errors will create their own neurological pathways through the brain, and stagnation or regression will set in as opposed to the desired improvement. In order to develop a skill, repetition must be accompanied by the clear intention to improve. Every psychic exercise designed to increase your psychic ability must be done with this intention. Repetition for the sake of repetition will not result in growth. In fact, repeating the same actions and expecting different results is a definition of "insanity"! Therefore, the rationale behind setting a clear intention grows even more important when applied to a psychic task.

# WAYS TO STRENGTHEN YOUR PSYCHIC ABILITIES

Think about when you learned to ride a bike. Perhaps you experienced trepidation. You may have known everything you were expected to do: watch the road, use your feet for the pedals, engage your sense of balance, and steer using your hands. You were taught that you had five senses: sight, smell, hearing, taste, and touch. In acquiring this new skill, you also realized you had a sense of balance and velocity. Perhaps you felt the wind on your skin as you moved through space and time. Here, you learned that you could also feel unseen things. And once you gained your sense of balance, you never lost it. Your growth was yours to keep. You also gained a new sense of freedom, as your new skill allowed you to travel farther and faster and independently, more so than ever before. In overcoming fear and by being persistent, you gained not only a new skill but also new levels of sensory perception.

Strengthening your psychic abilities in order to become a rune caster is very similar to learning how to ride a bike. You can read all the books there are about bike riding, but you are never going to truly understand it until you attempt it yourself. Visualization, meditation, and maintaining an open mind are all ways that you, as a magick practitioner, can strengthen and improve your psychic abilities.

## Visualization

A large part of rune reading as well as divination in general is learning to see beyond what can be readily perceived by the eyes or imagined in the mind. Whether your practice is spiritual or secular, you can begin by using creative visualization in order to accentuate your psychic abilities. Before you are able to see and interpret messages, you need to be skilled at visualization.

You can begin by visualizing anything. Create a picture in your mind of something familiar, such as a favorite food or a piece of fruit. Imagine it in excruciating detail. Try to "see" its color, shape, texture, depth, dimension, light reflection, relative size, and all other aspects of an object that make it "real" in your mind. Be as specific as you can.

Once you have mastered visualization, add another layer of sensory perception. If you can visualize an ice cream cone, try visualizing and experiencing its temperature. If you can visualize a flower, add the sensory perception of scent. Then try a more complex visual like a lotus flower. See if you can orient your mind to the point where you are able to count the petals and notice the gradations of color saturation in individual lotus petals. Then progress to picturing the surroundings of the lotus. Can you feel the temperature of the water in which it's floating? Is the water still, or does the surface ripple?

Create the ability to see the unseen by first using the power of visualization of known objects. Next, apply your honed skill to the unseen realm. You can engage with a known memory with as much detail as your mind will permit. Then you will continue to build and apply this skill to emotions. Begin with things that you know well; your final progression will be to apply this skill to unknown things. Try something that you can verify. Visualize the number of rooms in the home of someone you know. Then you can check with that person to see if your vision is accurate. Also check in with yourself to see if you get any internal messages or feelings as to whether you are correct or not.

Practice visualizing the runes. Trace their staves with your mind's eye and see if you can engage your other senses while doing so. Is it possible for you to picture them and hear them at the same time? Listen and see if they speak to you. Each rune has a sound, and you may discover that they have a message for you as well. Build upon your visualization practice incrementally. Eventually, you will improve your psychic abilities, no matter what level of psychic talent with which you began.

## Meditation

Meditation is a way to quiet your mind and empty your brain of thoughts that can serve as distractions to psychic development. In meditation, you center your consciousness around your body and your breath, allowing yourself to focus on the simple exchange of energy between yourself and your environment.

As you focus on your breath, the cycle of energy is released and replenished; you may find it difficult to disengage from random thought. Keep practicing. By training your mind to empty itself of thoughts, you are creating room for psychic awareness. It is far more difficult to access an oracle if you are mired in the demands of mundane life. Meditation is an excellent way to begin that separation from the mundane world and pass into the realms of magick.

When you establish a meditative practice, do so with the intention of making head space for things like psychic awareness and clairvoyance. Dedicate time to be still and quiet. Meditation need not be lengthy at first. Small successes are still successes. In the beginning, you may experience racing thoughts instead of absence. The "emptying" of ideas comes first. Allow the thoughts and stresses of life to fall away as you focus on your breathing.

Some witches find guided meditations helpful. Guided meditations are read aloud by another person or are prerecorded and played while the practitioner attempts to get into a relaxed state. Relaxation, however, is not the goal of meditation. It is a by-product. In a meditative state, your awareness is heightened, not lessened. You are energized because you are focusing on the cycle of your breath and replenishing oxygen to every cell in your body. Meditation should feel enlivening and awakening, not sleep inducing.

## Opening the Mind

"Open-minded" is a term that gets bandied about quite a lot, but what does an open mind entail?

- An open mind is accepting.
- An open mind can entertain possibilities.
- Most importantly, an open mind is a mind that is able to receive.
- In order to develop an open mind, it is necessary to explore and confront inherent biases that every individual has. Whether we care to admit it or not, we are all shaped by the experiences chosen or wrought upon us by our life path. Maintaining an open mind requires a certain level of unattachment to outcomes.

You may find working with runes challenging and frustrating at times. Examine your responses to discover if you were hoping for something you did not see or if you could not accept what the oracle was showing you. Having expectations is not a problem in and of itself. It is when those expectations interfere with psychic development that they become problematic. If the runes are instructing you in such a way that makes you uncomfortable, examine your discomfort. See if you can pinpoint the source of your reaction. While no one particularly enjoys being told "no," or learning that a desired outcome may not manifest as soon as they'd like or that a relationship appears to be ending, there is a value to sitting with uncomfortable information and allowing it to settle.

Even if you receive a disturbing message, remain open to the possibility that this is not a guarantee that some disaster will befall you. If you remain open-minded, you will be able to see the value of a well-timed warning. Harbingers of things to come can lead us in the right direction, even to the point where they may be avoided altogether. This is one of the benefits of cultivating an open mind. When you shut down and think to yourself, "No, that's wrong," you miss the opportunity for the lesson at hand.

## Combining Techniques

Once you have practiced visualization, meditation, and opening your mind as exercises in isolation, and after you have added some layer of complexity to each exercise (for example, a more complex visualization that activates numerous sensory perceptions, or the ability to sustain a meditative state for a prolonged amount of time, along with the ability to suspend the impetus for disbelief and accept your own intuition as a form of reality), then you are ready to combine these three techniques. Practicing the skills one by one will develop and improve them, as long as your focus and your intention are to improve. Then make a leap in your psychic development by combining them.

## Psychic Exercise

One way to practice combining psychic exercises involves using your clairvoyant abilities. Developing clairvoyance means that you are practicing your powers as a witch to see things that are not perceptible to others. You will begin with yourself, learning things about yourself that may be otherwise imperceptible. Once you have successfully done this, then you may branch out and try applying your skill to other people, situations, or objects.

Begin with a meditation. In the meditation, your sole focus is to clear your mind of mundane thoughts. Begin in a comfortable seated position, one that you can maintain. Breathe deeply from your diaphragm (the muscle in your abdomen) so that your upper body and shoulders do not move. Close your eyes and focus only on your breath. Chant a mantra if that helps you focus. Your mantra should align with the task at hand: becoming an adept rune reader.

Choose a single rune or a bindrune to focus on and use either the name of the rune or the pronunciation of the bindrune as a mantra. Once your mind is clear, remain in the meditative state and then begin your visualization.

Visualize your aura. It surrounds you on all sides. Picture your aura close to your body, like a second skin made of light. Envision it in detail. Notice gradations of color and slight changes in temperature. When the vision of your aura becomes very clear, the next step is to manipulate it.

Continue experiencing your aura as a second skin. It emanates from your physical body, but it is also external to your physical body. You use your skin to experience touch. You will use your aura to touch the unseen. Allow yourself to visualize and then feel your aura permeating your body and extending outward into your environment.

Now that you have engaged your sensory perceptions in your meditative state and have envisioned your aura in great detail, attempt to project it away from you to encompass things just out of reach. It's almost as though you are reaching for something, yet you remain still and in your meditative state. Use your voice to center yourself around your mantra if you feel your mind start to wander. Your aura can extend in all directions in front, above, behind, and below you. Choose a direction and focus on your ability to feel through your aura. You may experience a temperature change. You may get a new vision in your open mind. You may discover what is beneath your floorboards or the secrets that your walls contain. Listen intently to the information that is coming through the field of light that you have projected. When you have attained a sensation, information, or other type of affirmation, call your aura back to yourself and allow yourself to return to the present moment.

Use your grimoire to record your mantra, the details about your aura (color, texture, temperature, etc.) and your experience with reaching beyond. Keep working at the combining exercise and then use it to focus specifically on runes. Divine the answers you seek with confidence and ability.

# HOW TO PREPARE FOR CASTING RUNES

Now that you've familiarized yourself with rune basics such as which system you desire to work with and what type of spread you want to do, it is time to begin the work of engaging with the oracle in earnest. As with any worthwhile endeavor, preparation is necessary. If you do not properly prepare, you will not get the full benefit of the experience. Just as in herbal magick, before creating a spell or charm, you gather ingredients and prepare yourself mentally. You must prepare the environment as well. You want to work within a space that is conducive to a psychic experience.

### Choosing Your Space

Begin by choosing your space. If you are new to reading runes, you will benefit from taking the time to understand how your body feels and how it interacts with your environment. Think about the surface you will use. Chances are you will want to dedicate some time to rune reading, so make sure that the place you choose is comfortable enough. You may want to feel grounded and sit on the floor or even outdoors upon the earth, but you will still need a surface to work with. A cleared table or altar space and a chair or mat that is appealing will serve well. Do not sit on the ground if this position makes you uncomfortable. Your physical discomfort will draw your focus away from your reading.

### Preparing Your Space

Once your space is chosen, prepare it by removing mundane distractions. This may mean facing away from a wall clock, shutting down a computer, or silencing a phone. Create an air of stillness so that your senses are not pulled in different directions. While some ambient noise can be desirable, make sure it is as serene an environment as possible. The fewer distractions, the more open your mind will become.

Next, consecrate your space or make some informal declaration either silently to yourself or through a simple ritual that indicates to your subconscious mind as well as (or instead of, if you are not a spiritualist) to cosmic or divine entities that you are entering a serene and sacred space. Interacting with your environment with the intention of making it conducive to communication will allow you to achieve better results. A casual preparation will yield casual results.

Pay attention to the colors around you. Use a special or dedicated cloth, and handle it as though it were valuable. Light candles to activate some ambience or as a beacon of light by which insight may find you. Perform a smoke clearing with burned herbs to change the surrounding energy. Keep a grimoire, book of shadows, or journal nearby to record your spread and the interpretation. Put out a dish of salt in honor of the earth. A stick of incense, a cup of water, and a lighted candle are all that are necessary to create a hearth where communion and communication may take place.

## Choosing Your Query and Preparing Yourself

Once your environment is in order, it is time to prepare yourself. Hold your runes in their pouch or in the box in which they are stored. Close your eyes and hold them at heart level. If your runes are in a pouch, you can even hold them against your heart. You may feel your heartbeat creating a vibrational energy link between the runes and your corporeal body. This is good. Breathe into this feeling of vibration and heartbeat. Focus on your breath and your heartbeat and let everything else fall away from your mind.

When your mind is clear, allow yourself to engage with your runes. You have established a link through blood and breath, your heartbeat and life force. Now it is time to decide on the spread and ask your question.

Begin by touching the runes. You can do this with your eyes closed, feeling their texture or running your fingers over them, depending on how you store them. As you engage your sense of touch, you will speak your question out loud. Make sure your question is clear. You can use open-ended question words such as "what" or "which" to start.

### Asking the Question

Begin with a single question; otherwise it may be difficult to discern which part of your question the runes are responding to. If your question is to bring insight to a choice, then phrase your question with "what" or "which," such as "What is the likely result if I choose [scenario one]?" or "Which course of action will lead me to [desired scenario]?"

Formulate the question clearly in your mind, and when you are crystal clear, speak the question aloud. Since runes are a language, it is important that your query travels on a vibrational level through them. This is true even when you progress to reading someone else. There is a tendency to keep queries secret and let the oracle do all the work. While this is not inherently incorrect, your interpretation as a rune reader will be more useful the more information you have. Silent queries can also be a sign of distrust; either the questioner does not want their question heard, or the questioner is "testing" the oracle to see if it can answer without the benefit of them externally revealing the query. This indicates a closed or blocked mind.

If you or the person you are reading is coming from a place of skepticism, it is likely that they will not receive as accurate a reading as they might wish for, because they are not truly open to it. Questioning takes a certain amount of bravery. Words both written and spoken have a huge amount of power, because in the act of speaking or writing, you are creating change. In speaking, you are creating wave frequencies of sound that allow information to travel through space. In writing, you are creating a physical transformation on the page that can endure for generations. Acknowledge and appreciate this power. With your question clear and resonating in the space around you, it is time to reveal your answer.

# HARNESSING AND INTERPRETING ENERGY

Whether you choose to pull your runes one by one, grab a handful and sort them out, toss them at random, or swirl them around and around, you are creating and engaging with a field of energy. Like the heartbeat and breath connection that you established in your preparation, you are creating another connection. This one is tactile and kinetic. Pulling or drawing runes is deliberate. Tossing or throwing is more chaotic. Swirling is a method of invoking change.

To swirl your runes, you will need a smooth surface on which to work. Place your runes facedown in such a way that you can cover all of the runes with both hands. Then move your left hand in a clockwise motion, carrying the covered runes along with the movement, while your right hand moves counterclockwise. Allow runes to "escape" from one hand to another as you imbue them with the energy of your moving hands. You can stop when you feel the runes are ready to turn over. Sometimes, they will begin to spontaneously turn over and you can take this as your signal to stop. Any of these methods are useful and valid depending on your own needs. Sometimes you even need to physically shake things up before an answer will settle. The way in which you use your hands will be determined by what kind of energy you need to harness and align yourself with.

# FOCUSED ENERGY

If your intent or query requires focus, such as a need for clarity, then choose or draw your runes deliberately. If they are in a pouch, feel through the bag until a rune presents itself. You will know when a rune makes itself known. You will either be drawn to its silhouette, its surface, or its energy. Some runes will feel as if they are "falling away" while you gravitate toward the ones that are meant for you. Examine the form and meaning of the first rune you draw for alignment with your present state of mind.

If you are in accord, choose more runes until you have fulfilled the requirements of the spread that you have chosen. As you focus your energy, you may feel a "pull" from the runes, as if they are calling to you. You may also find yourself "drawn" to certain runes. The pull is a more active feeling, while being drawn toward a particular rune is more subtle. The feeling of a pull is the rune calling to you and making itself known, while the draw is your own subconscious mind calling to itself what it needs. Whether you feel a pull or a draw will depend on the nature or importance of the answer to your query.

Think about how you experience the world. You may be drawn toward a piece of art because you find it intriguing or pleasing. It captures your imagination and activates your mind. When something pulls you, it engages your heart and creates an emotional response. You can think of the distinction as the difference between knowledge (draw) and experience (pull), or even more simply, the draw is the domain of the mind and the pull is of the heart. Both energetic signatures are valid and you are likely to encounter either or both, and although they are similar, they are not the same.

## WHEN TO PULL AND WHEN TO THROW

With all of the choices and variables delineated in this chapter, some degree of introspection becomes necessary when deciding how to approach and interact with the oracle. You may not always know the correct method until you arrive at the gate. This is why it is helpful to understand the different methods of storing, choosing, and drawing, as well as the types of spreads and interpretations. All of these different aspects of rune work are part of the whole: the rune cast and the rune reading and interpretation. Think about the many things that go into creating this whole experience of consulting an oracle and determine the correct path that is the most authentic to your practice. The type of witchcraft you practice will rightly impact these decisions. When to cast runes by deliberately choosing them by pull or draw or by throwing them will depend on everything from how you feel most comfortable engaging with the oracle to the types of runes you are using as well as the type of material that your runes are inscribed upon.

This choice is both psychic or spiritual and practical. For example, there are several rune sets on the marketplace described as "crystal," but they are actually glass! Glass should never be thrown, because the runes will chip and you probably would not enjoy handling shards of glass. Ogham runes are often scribed on slender lengths of wood or on twigs, and it can be very satisfying to close your eyes, choose three or five or ten with your intention, mix them up, toss them, and see how they fall at random. Whether you choose the precise number of runes for your desired spread from the whole group one by one or select a grouping and throw them is largely determined by your own energetic state and/or the nature of your query. If you wish to change your state of mind, choose the opposite approach. For example, if you are in a focused state and you need to feel more unbridled, use the random method. If your energy is chaotic and you need to focus, choose deliberately one by one. Ceramic runes could be pulled or tossed, but runes scribed on certain stones will be too heavy to throw. Also, these acts of pulling and throwing are energetically different.

A throw has an element of chaotic or random energy to it. This can be useful when seeking guidance for when you feel particularly stuck and need direction. A pull is more deliberate and is a better method if there is a choice that needs to be made. Your actions should align with your intentions, and when to pull and when to throw will be determined by your needs.

# CASTING THE RUNES

If you use an altar, keep your runes facedown and covered with a cloth, then choose based on your instinct and attraction without knowing which rune you are choosing. For a three- to five-rune spread, you can pull them directly from their container and place them in the order in which they were chosen. Alternately, you can lightly toss them onto a special soft cloth or into the lid of their storage box, noting their relative position to each other to determine the meaning of placement, then turn them faceup. If you are doing a more complex spread, you can choose each rune blindly but deliberately while whispering each position. The type of spread you wish to perform, the depth of information that you require, and your state of mind will help determine what sort of rune pull or throw you should do. Are you seeking clarity and order for a complex situation? Pull, turn, or draw your runes one at a time. Are you feeling impulsive, spontaneous, and energetic? Toss a few to align your runes with your state of being. Different methods will be appropriate at different times, and as you get accustomed to handling your runes, your practice will grow.

By handling your runes, you will grow to know them intimately. You may find that you begin to recognize individual runes by touch alone and that you feel compelled to throw them in order to retain a certain level of detachment. You also may find that if you are using carved runes, you might eventually know them so well that you are able to read them blind and won't even need to physically see them because you will understand their symbolism through touch alone.

No matter which method you use in choosing runes for a spread, you are making a choice, and it should be deliberate with some kind of clear rationale or justification behind it.

# BEFORE DRAWING RUNES

Part of your preparation should be spent interacting with your runes without asking them a question. Your first impulse might be to clear and "reset" your runes by wafting burned herbs around them or laying them facedown on a dish of salt. These simple ritual suggestions create an air of importance around the experience of the rune spread. Before you bring your queries to the runes, try mixing them up and rearranging them a little bit first to see how they feel. The runes may give you a signal about when it is time to stop mixing and when it is time to start questioning. If your question is clear to you prior to beginning, you can engage in a brief meditation as you mix up the runes. Think of the origin of your runes—not how you acquired or created them, but how they came into being. Acknowledge them as a source of power and communication and tell them. They are your conduit to the oracle. Approach them with a clear intention and always with respect.

## *Change Energy*

If it is a shift in circumstance or situation that you seek, you may need to engage with runes in a different way. Take them out of their container and lay them facedown on a smooth surface. Close your eyes and place your hands lightly upon all of the runes and begin moving them with your hands, starting with your left hand in a clockwise motion and your right hand in a counterclockwise motion. Swirl the runes around as you speak your question out loud.

When you feel the energy of the question permeate the runes, they may ask you to stop moving. Come to a point of stillness and then open your eyes. See which runes have turned themselves over and see to which one your eye is drawn first. If no runes have turned over spontaneously, hold your hands directly over them and tune in to the one you feel or touch first without "trying" to touch any one in particular. Start with the first rune that calls your attention and read its significant meaning. If it aligns, choose or turn over more runes until you have satisfied the correct number for the spread you have chosen to do.

### Chaotic Energy

Sometimes we are confronted by sudden and unexpected change. This can be harnessed in the energy of a rune cast by literally shaking them up. You can shake your runes in their pouch or cup them in your hands to mix them. Then you can select a few and drop or gently toss them on a cloth and see which one hits the surface first. Create an energy that is aligned with your situation and feel how the energy shifts once you have manipulated it. Refer to modern interpretations and proceed with your spread.

# DIFFERENT KINDS OF RUNE CASTS

The different kinds of techniques for choosing runes previously described are all appropriate to use, depending on the nature of your question and your personal feelings in the moment. Experimenting with different methods of casting runes will strengthen your ability to feel subtle energies. Once you have established your method of engaging with runes, you are ready for the next steps in rune casting. The order of rune casting along with the accompanying variables are listed in order in the following list:

1. **Preparation:** physical and emotional space. Variable: Immediate surroundings and immediate needs.
2. **Query:** open-ended. Variable: Spoken or written or both.
3. **Cast:** total number of runes. Variable: Pull, throw, or turn.
4. **Spread:** arrangement. Variable: Relates to depth of question.

5. **Interpretation:** reading. Variable: Modern or traditional meanings.
6. **Reflection:** integrating new information. Variable: Recorded insight or ephemeral.

Follow these steps for successful rune casts. Memorizing the key steps is important. You might not always have time to be as thorough as the runes would prefer, but as you become adept, you will learn which parts lend themselves to truncation and which do not. A successful rune cast can mean that the runes reveal information that is accurate or challenging. It can be affirming and inspiring. It could also contain a warning. Rune casting is a practice. The more you practice, the more confident you will become.

# PART III

# RUNE MAGICK

Runes can be used as talismans as well as an oracle. In Part III, you will learn how to incorporate runes into sigil work by practicing repeated symbolic patterns that will give your magick practice strength and clarity. Linear runes are particularly adaptable to candle magick. You will learn how to select the right candle and scribe, as well as how to prepare stencils so that your rune carvings are precise and effective. And templates for magick rune meditation focal matrices will be explained.

## Chapter 8

# RUNES TO USE FOR SIGILS INDICATING TRANSFORMATIONS, GATEWAYS, AND GROWTH

It is possible to use runes for more than just divination. You can incorporate runes into spells and charms as powerful aids to achieving a magickal goal. You don't need to only pose questions to runes. Runes have highly magickal associations that go beyond their oracular properties. As symbols of power, runes can protect, attract, or repel. Understanding the different magickal applications to which runes are adaptable opens up new possibilities for incorporating runes into a practice of witchcraft.

One of the early uses of runes was in the form of labels. Using runes to describe objects infuses the objects with mystery. You can observe this easily by taking a candle and doing something as simple as carving the word "candle" on it in runes. See the transformation yourself: The candle takes on the air of mystery and importance just by bearing its own name in runes.

# RUNES FOR MANIFESTING AND INVOKING

Runes are powerful tools for calling things into being. Using runes as a point of focus either as a mantra repeated during a meditation or spoken aloud during a spell can sharpen your focus and intention. Having a clear intention is essential in spellcraft. When you use runes in spellcraft, you are creating a new and desirable reality according to your will. Identifying runes that will lend their aid to you will enhance your craft.

As you learned in Chapter 2, the Norse rune Mannaz is often used to depict the self. As also outlined earlier, Jēra, a rune of patience, is representative of abundance, and Kaunaz contains the power of opening. Working with these three runes together is an excellent starting point for a powerful manifesting spell. There are many ways to incorporate these runes into your craft. First, learn them. Memorize their character and attributes. Ancient associations correlate to the self, the harvest, and fire.

### Mannaz

Mannaz is representational of the self, which could be a call to you to focus on your own self-care.

Other modern associations include self-empowerment, belief in one's own abilities, and an acceptance of a level of self-worth wherein the practitioner believes they deserve the benefits of magick, are powerful enough to invoke them, and are wise enough to appreciate them.

### Jēra

Jēra is associated with harvest. Today, harvest means having enough. What is enough? That is for you to decide. You are allowed to have needs and are deserving of having those requirements fulfilled. Harvest contains all the sustenance and the rewards of hard work— everything that you have coming based on the amount of effort you have invested in your endeavors. Jēra is abundance. Perhaps this is an abundance of time in which to pursue creative endeavors. It could signify material comfort and an end to deprivation. Jēra can signify money, wealth, comfort, or all three.

## Kaunaz

Kaunaz is not just fire, but a transformational opening. Like fire, this opening can grow if it is properly tended and if conditions are right.

### Setting Up Runes for Manifestation

Select these three runes and place them on your altar in an inverted triangle configuration. This is a different type of magick than rune casting. For manifesting and invoking, you do not select runes through the hand of fate or by chance. You choose them consciously, knowingly, and with a clear intention. This should be something or some situation that you require in your life in the near future, no more than one year out or not past the end of the calendar year or culmination of the Wheel of the Year.

The rune at the point of the triangle is Mannaz. Above Mannaz and to the right is Jēra, and to the left of Jēra is Kaunaz. In placing the runes in this triangle formation and allowing yourself to enter a trancelike state while gazing on them, you will hold in your mind the following images and ideas to bring power to your work:

- You, represented by **Mannaz**, are the foundation of the work. You call your own will into being to manifest and show forth in the world the highest opportunity and best possible outcome for the challenge or obstacle at hand. Notice that the patterns of Jēra and Kaunaz are both contained within Mannaz. Everything that you need, all that you require, already dwells within you.

- Your task is to make it visible, tangible, and observable on the earthly plane. **Jēra** will help you do that. Be clear in what you are seeking. The more specificity and clarity you can envision, the greater your success will be.

- Finally, **Kaunaz** will help you set it into motion. In its aspect of opener, use Kaunaz to create an opening in the field of dreams so that you are creating a mental construct of having room for what you require. If a door is closed, persist in opening it. Try different angles. If a knock doesn't work, try a push or a key. These are all metaphors for different actions you can take.

In order to create an opening in the field, it is imperative to take action. A spoken charm, however beautiful or clever, will not do it alone. Neither will the most disciplined of trance techniques. It is a combination of all these powers, the confluence of intention and action, that will allow you to manipulate the field and create the opening that you need in order for the correct outcome to enter into observable reality. This means that your success is known not only to yourself but to others as well. It can be both unprecedented and undeniable.

Using the inverted triangle formation is important because it creates a visual vessel on which you may focus, almost like a funnel. Envision your needs being met, your desires fulfilled, and this manifestation flowing into your life. The inverted triangle is also the alchemical symbol for water. Use the energy of water to invite you manifestation. Water flows with great force and contains great power. Its strength cannot be contained, but it can certainly be channeled. Empower yourself to speak aloud the manner in which your desires should manifest and allow the runes to represent that vision. It could be an influx of money or recognition for work you have done. It could be demonstrated affection or a promotion, or any other type of success that you feel would benefit from a magickal influence. Center your mind around the ancient script of runes, the transcendent language that has endured through the ages, and give yourself the power that they contain to augment your will and bring about your heart's desire.

# RUNE STACKING TO CREATE A PORTAL

Runes can be deliberately selected in order to create an opening. In rune reading, you engage with an oracle to gain information and insight by drawing from a collection of runes, but usually drawing blind. This means that you don't know prior to casting with which runes you'll be engaging.

Stacking runes is different. You're intentionally choosing specific runes in order to activate or accelerate a desired outcome. Furthermore, you don't set out the runes in a traditional spread; instead, you stack them if they are tiles or wood slices, or balance one on top of the other if they are sticks.

Rune stacking combines a spoken intention with a physical act to create an energetic alignment between you and your intention. A thought becomes a word or chant. And when the word is accompanied by an action, the energy of the spell is increased. If your runes are scribed or carved on tile or stone, you are creating a miniature cairn. The cairn is used by travelers to guide others. Think of rune stacking as building a cairn so that you are able to direct unseen energies. The cairn represents the direction you want things to turn, which is to shift an outcome in your favor.

Placing runes with intention is one technique in using and understanding rune magick. Continuing to work with Mannaz, Jēra, and Kaunaz, preferably on stone, tiles, or wood slices, place Mannaz at the bottom, Kaunaz in the middle, and Jēra on top. This represents your rightful abundance flowing through the opening uninterrupted and landing square in the core of your being. By balancing the stones or tiles, you are imbuing the tiny cairn with your intention, which is a signal to the universe. Stacking stones indicates the correct path, especially when there is a turn in the path. Your tiny cairn is a small but powerful observable indicator of where and how you want your outcome to manifest. Its beauty and power are contained within its relative simplicity: abundance, through here, to me. You can even repeat the pattern like a mantra:

JĒRA, ABUNDANCE!
KAUNAZ, OPENING!
MANNAZ, ALL FLOWS TO ME!

Creating the cairn with runes is an indicator to the powers (elemental, celestial, angelic, ancestral, or whichever you typically engage with) that you are committed to your path, that you are on the right track. The cairn is also temporary. It is your guidepost reminding you to act in accord. If you are trying to manifest a new job or a promotion, the visible cairn on your altar reminds you to write and distribute your resume and build your network. If you wish to manifest a passing grade, the cairn is your study reminder. When your challenges have been met, your lessons learned, and your blessing manifested, you can easily dismantle the cairn, return your runes to your set, and give thanks for the abundance that is rightfully yours, that flows to you, that is part of you and belongs to you.

## Stacking on a Vertical Axis

Another form of stacking is along a vertical axis. Keeping the same order with Mannaz at the bottom, Kaunaz in the middle, and Jēra on top, line up the runes and then draw them stacked close together on a small piece of carboard, about the size of a business card. The size of a business card or credit card is symbolic because this particular shape follows the ratio of the Golden Mean.

The Golden Mean is a repeating pattern found in nature, and it is also an Aristotelian concept of balance. In philosophy, the Golden Mean is the middle path between polar opposites or extremes, and its sentiment is in alignment with the concept of moderation as a desirable practice. In mathematics, the Golden Mean can best be described as the relationship between two parts of a line where the whole line and the longer segment have the same ratio as the relationship between the long segment and the short segment. It is inherently pleasing to the eye and carries within it the divine patterns that recur throughout the planet in many life forms. You can observe the Golden Mean many places in nature, including the spiral of seashells, the arrangement of sunflower seeds in the blossom, and the pattern of a pine cone. You can observe the Golden Mean in architecture both ancient and modern, in structures such as the Parthenon in Greece as well as the credit or debit card in your pocket.

Stacking Mannaz, Kaunaz, and Jēra is more effective for manifesting and invoking because these runes do not readily share a common stave. Keep the drawing of the stack runes where you can engage with it frequently (for example, next to your banking card). Get used to the concept of your desire and needs being met and act in accord as though they already are.

## Stacking with Ogham Runes

Ogham runes are all designed along a stave. You can use the Ogham runes with the same sentiment of manifesting and choose which ones to stack depending on if you want to organize them by their esoteric meaning or by creating a transliteration of your desire. If there is something specific you want to achieve, take a small piece of cardboard shaped like a credit card (so it follows the Golden Mean) and draw a vertical line lengthwise through the middle. Then draw the appropriate runes. For example, an esoteric stack of Ogham runes

       *Part III: Rune Magick*

along a stave might include Duir for strength and power, Gort in its flowering aspect, and Coll for its encapsulated wisdom. With the associative stave on one side, you can then transliterate your intention on the other side. Can you refine your intention into a single word and spell it out for yourself? Some suggestions include:

- Healing
- Forgiveness
- Clarity
- Union

- Success
- Victory
- Safety

Remember when creating staves with Ogham runes, they are stacked from the bottom up. Any transliteration that you attempt should begin with the first letter at the bottom.

Once your card has been created, you have several options on how to use it. It can remain on your altar for as long as you need it. If you are attempting a money draw or need to manifest wealth, carry the card in your wallet. If it is healing and health you are seeking to amplify, carry it on your physical person, in a pocket or a shoe. If there are dreams you want to manifest, keep it under your pillow.

Rune stacks inscribed on cards are discreet, ephemeral, aesthetic, indecipherable to most, and can also be gifted if there is something you want to manifest for another person. This is a versatile application of runes in a very modern way.

# CREATING SIGILS WITH RUNES

Sigils are used in occult practices, particularly for spells and charms. Runes can be easily incorporated into sigil work by providing a foundation upon which new and original sigils can be built. This adds a layer of protection and secrecy, for although runes are well known and recognizable, the meaning of a sigil is meant only for the individual who created it and it does not have to carry meaning to anyone else.

Of course, there is nothing to prohibit the sharing of effective sigils, but sigils are deeply personal. Although there are enduring sigils of proven efficacy and accepted power, sigils can also be original and therefore are also ephemeral by nature. Sigils are often crafted individually and are uniquely suited to the specific task or spell at hand.

Sigils have been used on magick coins and in magick squares. They represent the mysteries of Heaven and the celestial powers. They are conduits that unite practitioners with metaphysical celestial energy. This gives them an inherent affinity with runes. Like runes, sigils demand to be touched, and their evolution has ranged from high-touch amulets to valuable curios. Carrying sigils on your person, in a pocket, or in a purse or displaying them behind glass or as a part of altar craft are all authentic and appropriate ways to interact with sigils.

A sigil is essentially a monogram: the alphabetic representation of desire, scribed in overlapping letters, usually within the border of a circle or square, in order to create a new and distinct single letter. The act of creating the sigil imbues it with magickal energy. This energy is attributed to a single source of power that is external. It will manifest differently to different types of witches. For example, some witches will experience the energy as spirit or deity, or even angelic. Some may experience it as a planetary vibrational energy in a similar way that some people are governed by the stars of the constellation in which the sun appeared to traverse on the day they were born. Whether you commune with Goddess or God, angel or ancestor, spirit of nature or music of the sphere, the sigil is your tangible key with which to unlock a sacred and powerful mystery.

More than symbols, sigils, like runes, also have sound due to their alphabetic, albeit cryptic, nature. It is unlikely that a sigil can be truly understood by anyone other than its maker. The core components of the sigil are:

- **The sound:** that which we experience as audible vibrational energy or waves
- **The character:** the unique pattern that we are able to understand through sight
- **The idea:** the profound imagining of the magickal mind inscribed within
- **The actual representation:** the witch's ability to see beyond

If you have any doubt of your ability to see beyond, this is inherent to your intellect and can easily grow quickly as long as you continue to cultivate your psychic sight. Just like any other skill, when you practice your psychic sight repeatedly and with the intention to improve, you will gain skill. First, think about the psychic abilities that you already possess and build from there. For example, you are already able to interact with language and symbol. You may ponder the word "cat": a short series of symbols that represent sounds when combined and create several mental images. First, there is the arrangement of the symbols themselves that allow you to "hear" them in your mind. Consequently, there are the individual meanings and sounds as well as the word that these letters make. The word has its own shape, its own meaning beyond the individual letters. And within that combination, there are thousands of accompanying images.

Say the word "cat" while opening your mind, and you will experience a wide-ranging mystical journey that may begin in ancient Egypt as priestesses dance at the feet of Bast. The word may then carry you to familiar spirits you have known: playful kittens, lean hunters, childhood pets, and everything in between. Think of the effortlessness of the infinite energy and images you have just experienced and understand that this level of details was perceived and experienced through the grace of three simple characters that activated the schema you had already accumulated. Your next step is to apply that same skill to runes. You have just proved to yourself that you can get mental messages from symbols and "see" things that the symbols represent. Now that you understand that you already possess the skill of using symbols to see beyond, you will be able to transfer the skill to rune reading.

### Express a Basic Concept

Begin by using runes to express a familiar concept or a simple state of being that you wish to amplify. For example, you can create your first runic sigil manifesting success by combining runic systems. Use the Witch rune for Harvest and inscribe it within a circle. Then use a transliteration of the word "reap" and add it to the design using Perthro, Ansuz, Ehwaz, and Raidō, read right to left. Thus, you have set your intention in both a pictographic and literal way.

You can use another application of runic synthesis if you wish to uncover a secret or reveal something. This sigil is especially useful if you suspect that someone is not being forthright or honest, or is concealing some kind of hidden motive. Scribe the Witch rune for Eye within a circle, and above it, use Thurisaz, Uruz, Raidō, and Teiwaz for a right-to-left transliteration of "truth."

Perhaps you have a need to heal a rift or strengthen a bond. You can use the Witch rune of the Rings inscribed within a circle. In the outer rings, draw the first initials of the names by which the two people you seek to unite are known. Then in the center ring, create a bindrune combining the two initials. This is a versatile sigil that can be dedicated in any number of manners (familial, platonic, or romantic bond) and can adapt to either Ogham runes or Elder Futhark runes.

One pattern you will notice when synthesizing sigils is that there is a guide contained within each one. The guide informs you of the action you must take in order to get what you need. For example, the manifesting sigil contains the pictographic Witch rune for Harvest. This is what you want: the rich and beautiful abundance that is your right as a wise steward of the earth who works magick for the benefit of all beings, the lush and bountiful fulfillment of all the heart's desire so that safety, comfort, ease of living, creative endeavors, a full heart, and a stocked cupboard are within arm's reach. Once you are able to envision this and you know what safety and comfort feel like, you can accept that experience as part of the "now" no matter what is dictated to you. Allow yourself to actually feel and experience your desired state, then turn your attention to the transliteration "reap."

This is what you must do in order to shift the world into resembling your vision (which is now clear). Action must be in accord with the vision. Anything that diverts your focus is to be weighed mightily lest you spend precious psychic resources enlivening things that you don't want. Train your mind while acting in accord and let your newfound skill of crafting sigils through synthesis enrich your practice.

### *If Someone Isn't Honest*

What if your intuition is telling you that someone is not being honest or forthright with you? You can summon guides to lead you to the correct answer or you can ask the truth to reveal itself. Whichever approach you decide to take, creating a sigil for seeing can add energy. Scribe the Witch rune for Eye in the center of a circle. Above it, inscribe the transliteration for "truth" by drawing Thurisaz, Uruz, Raidō, and Teiwaz, which will be read from right to left. Again, the guide function of this sigil is what you wish to reveal (scribed in the transliteration) and how you plan to do it (by employing your psychic sight). Since sigils are physical objects, you will want to use durable materials such as cardstock. You can also use air-drying clay and a scribe to create a sigil. The sigil can also be recorded in your grimoire, especially if it proves to be effective. If you do not feel your magick is powerful enough to aid in manifesting your needs within your time frame, you just may need more practice. Creating a sigil is a magickal art, but it is also a skill, and skills improve when they are practiced repeatedly and with the intention to improve upon them.

# ORDEALS AND OBSTACLES

The metaphysical meanings of runes extend far beyond their alphabetic and phonetic meanings. More than a literate system of communication, runes have transcended these boundaries to represent not only letters and sounds but also complex aspects of human existence. The discovery of the runes by Odin was through ordeal. A theme of hardship, even suffering, runs through the modern occult associations of runes, for difficulty is an inescapable part of life. In magick and witchcraft, ordeals and obstacles are accepted as necessary for spiritual growth. Magick is used to confront, integrate, dispel, or transform the constraints that impede the manifestation of desire.

If a rune spread reveals a bad omen, the witch need not be resigned to an unfavorable outcome. Rather, this is an indication that a challenge is at hand. This could materialize internally or externally. The obstacle could be emotional, or it could be mundane. Runes are tools that can provide guidance around these obstacles so that they can be integrated. To integrate an obstacle is to accept that with light, shadows also come. Witches lean in to this shadow so that it does not overwhelm or otherwise rule the prevailing energy. To deny the darkness is to deny balance itself.

Balance and the seeking of balance is a desirable state; however, a pendulum at rest does not reveal its secrets. Balance is often described as an "act." It has movement and energy. Balance is not a stagnant state. It is in the acceptance of disruption, the awareness of energetic subtleties, and the ability to accept and integrate the information and to move accordingly. It is the acceptance that into every life, rain must fall, and that the quest for balance means that there are naturally times when events will not be favorable and you will not be at your best.

When a negative outcome is revealed in a rune cast, the first thing the witch has to explore is where in the spread it comes up. This may indicate that a generational wound has surfaced and it is the need of the modern witch to confront the past. If the obstacle is indicated in the near future, then action can be taken in the here and now to stave off an undesirable outcome. In times of uncertainty and turmoil, decisions demand greater scrutiny. Introspection and acceptance are necessary in determining the appropriate steps.

Pulling a rune that indicates a disruption, an interference, or what could be perceived as a negative influence should be expected and not feared. In witchcraft, there has been much speculation on the origin of the word "witch," with some people persisting in the belief that it is etymologically connected to the word "change" or "bend." With this in mind, it is up to the witch to realize that any negative or unwanted influence, whether in the past or the future, can be changed. This is not to say that past events themselves can be changed; however, the manner in which the past affects the present can be altered.

### Dealing with Obstacles and Ordeals

Since the concept of an ordeal is inherent in the generative legend of the runes, accepting and integrating an ordeal or challenge is a crucial skill in becoming a rune-master. It is impossible to gloss over every difficulty and ignore portents and omens. Difficulties must be confronted, and engaging with the power of runes can be of great assistance. Instead of "light washing" an unfavorable outlook, lean in to it and be proactive. The runes may be calling you to examine and engage with your shadow self. The manner in which the shadow manifests is different in every person, but those who are able to lean in to the darkness may have a better chance at changing it.

How does this change occur? The change can be activated in several ways. Here are a few:

- **Dissipate:** One way is to dissipate. To dissipate an ordeal is to lessen its power. Try to make it less important.

- **Release:** The phrase "I release that which no longer serves me" is popular in witchcraft due to its succinctness.

- **Integrate:** Experiences that bring a lesson that can neither be dissolved nor released need to be integrated. This is a powerful step on the path to wisdom. It becomes a part of you, like a scar after a physical injury.

- **Transform:** An act of transmutation can create an energetic shift where you experience the ordeal differently. Instead of viewing it as a challenge, hail it as a teacher. Glean what you can. Actively look for the lessons and find an opportunity for growth even if you have to search for it.

- **Accept:** Some life events cannot be moved through without pain or anguish. Ordeal is a great teacher even though its lessons are harsh. There are times when even doing the "right" thing does not feel good. Rely on your moral code when intuition and control over your emotions fail you. When things don't *feel* right, accept your choices and take solace in that fact that at least you are *doing* right.

Ogham runes that are strongly associated with obstacles and ordeals are:

- Saille
- Uath
- Ruis

If you are experiencing an ordeal, you can strengthen your psychic resolve by engaging with one of these three runes and combining it with a stop. As you learn more about stops, you will also see how effective they can be when navigating an ordeal.

# CREATING A STOP

While much of spellcrafting centers around manifesting, there is also a need for its equal but opposite function, which is to create a stop. It is not realistic to think that the practicing witch will only ever need to call things forth. Magick can also be used to inhibit or delay things that are already set into motion. Plans change, desires change, and what seemed necessary or wanted may turn out not to be. There is wisdom in being very specific in both intention and action; however, the most carefully laid plans are not immune to outside forces, and there is only so much that one individual person can influence.

When an unintended consequence arises, the witch is not without power to affect these circumstances. By using a stop, a witch can redirect or change an impending situation. This magickal working can be applied to any number of necessary actions, including, but not limited to:

- **Stopping** a specific person from taking an action
- **Delaying** or interrupting a process that has already started

Again, specificity and clarity of intention are of utmost importance.

Ask yourself why you need to use the stop. For example, you may find that you sent a message to someone in error or that there is a high likelihood that communication will not be received with the meaning that was intended. While it may not be possible to unsend a text or recall an email, using a stop can help prevent unwanted situations from growing and keep them from commanding even more attention.

Perhaps in order for your peace of mind to remain intact, you need a certain message to go unnoticed. Being specific will make your stop more effective. Using runes as a stop can help deflect a misfire or quell a brewing storm.

Witches are also known for having an impact on the weather. Perhaps you have travel plans and you see poor conditions on the horizon. Either way, your original plan is going to have to change, so remaining flexible and using a stop can also be a way to maintain some semblance of control when you're not always in control. Perhaps you just want to stop a light rainfall from ruining your weekend plans. This is not to say that you want dominion over the forces of nature, but that you want to exert your own magickal influence to place a temporary stop on a minor inconvenience for a specified amount of time. It is not so different from the nursery chant, "Rain, rain, go away. Come again another day."

## Other Uses for a Stop

A stop can also be used in more serious matters. You may find that you need an undesirable health condition to shift, and while magickal workings are no substitute for medical attention, using a stop will never adversely affect the situation. Keep in mind that the placebo effect is well documented and that researchers are already very much aware that people have a proven ability to heal themselves when they believe they have taken an action that will accelerate the healing. This is true. The mind-body connection is something that we are barely able to understand, yet it has repeatedly been proven that it still exists independent of our understanding.

Using a stop is a way to center the mind so that intention and action remain in accord. Perhaps someone is bothering you and you want them to stop persisting in their action. Using a stop will serve as a powerful reminder not to participate in interactions that you do not want. First of all, the need to respond is something that you can control. You may experience patterns of communication that you need to break. A stop is a form of control, a galvanizing talisman that will help you focus your intent.

If the stop does not need to be permanent—and most stops are used for temporary effects—you can use ephemeral materials such as paper and candles. Even these should be chosen with care. For example, many witches like to use dragon's blood ink for spells. (Dragon's blood ink can be ordered online or purchased from your local New Age store.) This is because dragon's blood ink is associated with a special resin that has healing properties and adds another layer of intention to the stop. While dragon's blood ink might only resemble the resin by its color, it nonetheless has a connection. In addition to thwarting or warding off an undesirable outcome, dragon's blood will offer a measure of healing energy that may make the stop easier to bear.

To create a stop, you will need:

- A clear and specific intention of what you need to stop and for how long
- A straightedge
- A pen (selected with intention)
- Suitable paper, unlined

Begin with a double rune, using Isa both vertically and horizontally. This is to command a standstill in all directions. Your paper should resemble an equal-armed cross. Next you will draw Ehwaz, but in an inverted position. This is because of Ehwaz's association with the horse, the relationship between the horse and the rider, and forward momentum and movement. By inverting Ehwaz, you are creating a block. The movement and progression are called to cease. Finally, the apex of Ehwaz will become the touching triangles of Dagaz, the rune of transformations, so that unwanted energy is changed. Enclose the sigil within a circle to contain the energy.

## USING THE STOP

You may want to use the stop as part of a sigil. You can do this by scribing a circle and creating the stop inside of it or by scribing the stop and enclosing the circle around it. The circle is the symbol of containment in this application. The circle is used as a constraint. You can even begin by scribing the circle and writing within it the specific situation that you wish to stop. For example:

- Contact from [NAME]
- A message to [NAME]
- Rumors or gossip
- Bad dreams
- An infection
- A chain of events
- Plans you wish to cancel

Whatever it is that you need to put a stop to, enclose within the circle. Every time you write the intention, repeat the word "stop." You can even chant it as a charm, such as:

Movement cease.

Full stop.

Bring me peace.

Full stop.

Do not proceed.

Full stop.

Fulfill my need.

Full stop.

Whisper no word.

Full stop.

All goes unheard.

Full stop.

Silence unbroken.

Full stop.

My word has been spoken.

Full stop.

And by my own will.

Full stop.

This charm fulfill.

Full stop.

You can repeat the charm as you fill the circle so that the situation is perfectly contained. Then cover the circle with the stop. You can also dedicate a jar candle to the situation by carving a transliteration in runes and then placing the candle on top of the stop. You can also carve the stop directly onto the candle and place the circle underneath.

# Chapter 9

# USING RUNES TO INVOKE LOVE AND ABUNDANCE

As a system of prophecy, runes can bring messages from beyond about all of the good things to come. Pulling a rune of blessing gives us the opportunity to fully engage with the wonderful state of anticipation. Having something to look forward to is key to maintaining a positive outlook, even in times of distress. The advent of something new, the promise on the horizon, and any and all welcome experiences that dawn and bring with them the rose- and gold-tinged warmth of hope can fortify the soul and assuage past injuries. Using runes in creative ways can help us recognize the good that is right in front of us and especially the shift in consciousness that indicates more good things are coming into occurrence.

# RUNES AS HARBINGERS OF BLESSING

In the previous chapter, the presence of obstacles and their significance were brought to light. Many runes contain secret warnings; however, runes are not only to instruct on how to avoid danger; they also have numerous beneficial connotations and can bring with them prophecies of wonderful blessings. The meanings attributed to runes are meant to encompass wide arrays of human existence, and while warnings are always appreciated, there is also plenty of room for joy, union, fruitful partnerships, love, trust, harmony, beauty, and abundance. In the Witch rune system, the Star, Romance, the Rings, Harvest, and the Wave all bring elements of fulfillment and assurances of pleasure from the oracle. Sentiments and secrets can be written and recorded in the Theban alphabet if you are not ready to reveal your feelings. Using runes can be a form of protection when dealing with matters of the heart. When we love, we also risk and make ourselves vulnerable.

In the Elder Futhark Rune Row, several runes immediately stand out as positive omens. Gebō, Ingwaz, Wunjō, Berkanō, and Sowilo all bring immediate positive associations and indicate a favorable outlook in divination.

# THE LANGUAGE OF LOVE IN RUNES

Runes have always been used to show possession. A lot of their power lies in declaring a bond. For a quick and simple bonding ritual between lovers, create a bindrune simply by combining your initials along a vertical stave. Think of the way people sometimes carve their initials in trees as a symbolic token of bond and a declaration of love.

If you seek to be bonded to someone in a loving and fulfilling relationship, you must first become clear on what you have to give and what you hope to gain. Every relationship comes with a cost; there is some sacrifice that is inherent in union. Whether it is small and acceptable or too draining or otherwise untenable, you must be clear on boundaries and approach the following spell with utmost honesty.

# Manifested Bond

———— ❦ ————

A bond can be manifested, enhanced, or even healed with the bind-rune stave. For this spell, you will first need to create the bindrune for Love. The three Norse runes you will be working with are Wunjō, Gebō, and Ingwaz. Choose these three from your collection and place them vertically on your altar.

## You Will Need
- Pencil and paper
- Straightedge
- Pen with colored ink (red, green, or blue)
- Essential oil blend
- Cotton ball or pad
- 2" × 3" pouch made of muslin or similar cloth
- Bone or cowrie shell
- Iridescent gemstone such as moonstone, opal, labradorite, or quartz
- Match

## Directions
1. With the pencil and using something important for the straightedge, draw a vertical line down the center of your paper. At the top, make the angle for Wunjō, and underneath it, draw the × for Gebō so that the vertical line runs through the cross point of the arms of Gebō.

2. Underneath, draw Ingwaz in a way that the central aperture is not bisected by the stave and that the arms of Gebō touch the top of Ingwaz.

3. Once you've completed the drawing in pencil, go over it again in ink. Place this on your altar beside the vertical run of runes that you placed earlier.

4. Take the essential oil blend. It should be something that pleases you; determine the intensity and nature of your pleasure. Choose a scent that is either calming or arousing, depending on what type of energy you want this relationship to have. If you don't have an essential oil blend, use a drop or three of perfume, cologne, or whatever scent you find most pleasing.

5. Place a few drops on the cotton ball or pad and put the cotton imbued with scent into the pouch. Add the bone or cowrie shell (or one of each), the gemstone, and the match.

6. Finally, add the bindrune. If it is on paper, roll it up into a little scroll, or if you used rigid material like cardstock, just fold it so it fits.

7. Lightly hold the filled, scented, magickal pouch in your hands and rub your hands together to create friction and heat. Chant the names of the runes. Keep the pouch close to your body and next to your skin. You can wear it in the inside of your clothes by weaving a filament through the drawstring loops and keeping it around your waist or around your neck or elsewhere. You can keep it in your bed if this is where you want the partnership to manifest.

## *Simple Love Spell with Runes*

While some magickal workings are quite complex, others are simple yet can still yield results. Think of the investment of energy and time as commensurate with the result. If you perform a simple love spell, do not expect a marriage proposal, but certainly expect some positive and loving attention to be directed your way. A flirtatious glance or a welcomed text are all tangible results than can be brought about with the magickal use of runes. Here is a simple love spell you can do.

## You Will Need

- Railroad spike
- Red taper candle approximately 6" long
- Match
- Copal resin (readily available in most herb stores, particularly stores dedicated to magick)
- Mortar and pestle
- Attraction oil or an essential oil blend that is sensuous and appealing to you

## Directions

1. Decide on a rune system to use, either Elder Futhark or Ogham.

2. Use the railroad spike to create the staves that will form a transliteration of what you desire vertically on one side of the candle. Make the impression by pressing the tapered end of the spike into one side of the wax candle. Some examples are love, lust, and union.

3. On the other side of the candle, create a transliteration of the deity with which you have a strong connection and that is associated with love, such as Freya, Venus, or Eros. If it is a stable relationship you are seeking, use Hera. Names have power, and invoking a Goddess or God is customary for many witches. If this does not align with your practice or feels inauthentic or is not available to you, then just focus on what you want. The staves should be made with care but without hesitation. Study the forms so that you know what the stave should look like and remember if you are using Ogham, start from the bottom and work your way up.

4. Take the match and use it to remove any stray bits of wax so that the staves are clear.

5. Set the match and the candle aside and put a small amount of copal resin granules in your mortar and pestle and grind them up. As the larger pieces begin to break, think of communication barriers being broken. Whatever is keeping you from your desired experience can be changed. Allow your mind to envision any obstacles falling away; they are transmuted to dust by your magick and your will.

6. Pick up the candle and hold it over your mortar and pestle. Take pinches of the copal resin, which should now resemble a fine powder, and gently work it into the carvings. This will make them more noticeable, as the light color of the copal will contrast with the saturated tone of the red. As you touch the candle, think about the way you would like to be touched and use that energy to guide your actions. Is it a playful touch or a gentle touch that you seek? Mirror your desire by how you approach this task.

7. When the carvings are visible, take a drop of your chosen oil on your fingertip and use it to remove any excess dust from the copal that is lingering on the surface of the candle. Try to avoid getting the oil in the carvings, as the oil will cause the copal to darken and minimize the contrast. Your fingers will be pleasantly scented and sticky. Do not be afraid to get your hands dirty. Enjoy the scent, enjoy your craftwork, and when you are satisfied, use the match to light the candle and enjoy its seductive glow.

## RUNES AS ADORNMENT

Just as you consecrated a candle using runes, you can apply this same technique to your physical person. If you want to inspire sexy confidence, you can use your favorite essential oil blend and write your desires in runes on your own body. These intentions will not be visible to anyone, but you will know they are there. Even a simple transliteral rune for "touch" or "kiss" traced with your fingertip up and down your arms and legs or "hold" on your hand will prepare your body and mind to welcome sensuality. If it is an outward expression you are thinking, a simple liquid eyeliner can prove to be a useful medium for adorning the body with runes. If visibility is not something you are ready for yet, or if you are simply less inclined to do formal anointing with essential oil blends on yourself, you can also use moisturizer or foundation to scribe your desires on your person. These invisible but powerful gestures then become a part of your physical makeup and add a layer of magick to your grooming.

# COMMUNICATING WITH RUNES

Because runes are alphabetic, it is entirely possible to transliterate using runes. Communication is a key to any successful relationship. Giving voice to one's own needs comes with a certain amount of risk. Some risks are worth taking, but it is often impossible to know from the outset how things are likely to progress.

This is where the runes become invaluable. By creating a bind-rune, you are signaling your intention and injecting energy into the field of perceptible energy. For some people, this energetic frequency is not readily observable. People who spend no time developing their psychic abilities do not have them. Some people have a natural ability, but if it is not cultivated, an innate ability might not be particularly significant. The same is true of working with runes. Since runes are linguistic, they are vehicles of communication. They allow us to make meaning out of utterances and characters or symbols and expand our abilities to understand. Using runes to communicate is another application that will deepen your knowledge.

## Communicating a Need

Begin by first communicating with yourself. Identify one specific need or requirement and just focus on that. Next, draw the characters from the rune system with which you feel most comfortable working. Can you name what you need in the simplest terms? Can you communicate with yourself well enough to be able to simplify what it is that you need into a single word? Think first of the different dimensions of your life. These may include family, community ties, love, relationships, hobbies, spirituality, future goals, past debts, or other life situations or events. Think about what drives you and also what constrains you. Choose one, either a motivating factor or a constraint or obstacle, and see if you can refine it into a single word. Here are some examples:

- Time
- Health
- Love
- Travel
- Work
- Wealth
- Study

Notice that these words are intentionally short. This is because your next step will be to express them along a single stave. You are essentially beginning a dialogue with yourself by articulating either something you need or something you need to overcome. Use your grimoire and draw a single vertical line in the middle of a blank page. If you are using Ogham runes, start from the bottom and work your way up, transliterating a few into your own mother tongue. This is an exercise in using runes as a form of communication according to your current level of understanding, so it is not necessary to translate. Use your grimoire to outline your process. Here is an example:

- **Thought:** I need more time to accomplish my goals
- **Intention:** Goal (Here, you can be specific. Your goal can be anything. For example, if your goal relates to your magickal practice, your goal could be clairvoyance, mediumship, or channeling. It could also relate to your mundane life such as good grades or a new job.)
- **Constraint or challenge:** Time

Here is an example of what a stave for time might look like:

After you have created the stave and established a dialogue with yourself, the next level of communication is external and metaphysical. This means you will engage with either spirit, ancestor, deity, or the source of power that is connected to your modern practice. On this level of communication, you will formulate a request. Here are the steps:

- Identify and name the metaphysical level of communication (specific deity, name of ancestor, elemental energy, etc.)
- Establish the connection using a tool (mantra, *galdr*, pendulum, spirit board, etc.)
- Make a formal request for aid, insight, or prophecy

Once your intention and tools are ready, you may silently focus on the stave while you invoke metaphysical energy. Remember that Albert Einstein proved that time is relative and that the rate at which time passes is connected to your frame of reference. Einstein argued that time is an illusion and that the separation of the past, present, and future is not set; this theory has held up under experimentation. Remember the truth about what is known about gravity, space, and the passage of time and accept your own ability to exercise flexibility when manipulating time.

## Creating Sigils for Prosperity

Prosperity means existing with the state of having, being, and feeling a total absence of scarcity. Too often, the mind seizes on thoughts concerned with lack or emptiness, and unwittingly, this energy is amplified because it is receiving sustained focus and constantly gets reinforced. Using runes in sigils for prosperity is a potent way to shift this mindset. The prosperity sigil described here uses three runes from the Elder Futhark: Dagaz, Berkanō, and Jēra. Here is a way to create a sigil.

### You Will Need
- Cardstock, parchment, or some other type of high-quality paper
- Compass with pencil
- Paper money, folded
- Pencil
- Pen with green ink

### Directions
1. Inscribe on the cardstock a circle with a radius of approximately 1"–1¼". Use the compass to make as perfect a circle as you are able. The point of the compass will give you the center point of the circle.

2. Take the paper money (in as high a denomination as you are able to obtain) and fold it crisply so that you can use it as a straightedge.

3. Using the pencil, draw an × that crosses the center point of the circle and extends to the circle's edges. Connect the upper right point to the lower right point with a straight line, and repeat this same action on the opposite side, connecting the upper left point on the × to the lower left with another straight line. This will give you the energy of Dagaz, which can be interpreted as breakthroughs and transformations, centered within the border of a circle.

4. Incorporate Berkanō by first making a small dot on the midway point in the left vertical line. This dot should be directly left of the center point on the left side of Dagaz.

5. Draw two more dots, one at the midway point of the diagonal line that runs from the center point to the upper left and one in the midpoint of the diagonal line that extends from the center to the lower left.

6. Using the folded money as a straightedge, draw two diagonal lines extending from the midpoint on the left side of Dagaz to the upper and lower dots on the diagonals.

7. Incorporating the final rune, Jēra, is easy because the lower left angle is easily created by extending the lower diagonal line of Berkanō to the bottom of the circle. Then create the upper angle by starting at the top of the circle and drawing the "greater than" symbol.

8. Now you are ready to go over the sigil in green ink. Use the folded bill to retrace over all the pencil lines, provided you do not need to make any corrections or adjustments. Your runic prosperity sigil is now ready for use.

# USING THE RUNIC PROSPERITY SIGIL

The runic prosperity sigil can be used in two ways: as a talisman or as part of a spell. To use the sigil as a talisman, all you need to do is place it in your wallet. It can also be incorporated into a larger magickal working such as the following spell.

## *Money Drawing Spell*

Abundance and prosperity can take many forms. Increasing wealth by calling money to yourself is a practical and tangible application of the runic sigil. Once you have created it, you have essentially opened a portal through which magick and fulfillment will flow freely. This does not mean that it will occur without further effort. Think of the spell as the launching pad from which your desire will spring into being. By creating the sigil, you have only just begun. Of course, if you are not ready for more advanced magick or don't have time for a full spell, carrying the sigil near your currency will only benefit you in that it will help train your focus. However, if your intention is clear and you have a reasonable idea of further actions you could take and specific channels you can tap into, then proceed.

### You Will Need
- Runic sigil of abundance in green or black
- Bank statement, paycheck, contract, promise, or any document that is connected to the inflow of money
- Money of metal and paper; higher denominations are better, but any amount will do (multiples of three, five, and eight are particularly auspicious)
- 1 hagstone
- 1 crystal
- Effigy of power, either deity, natural, or something important to the witch
- Bell

## Directions

1. On your altar, place the sigil. On top of the sigil, you will place your document. On top of the document, place the currency. On top of the currency, place the hagstone. On top of the hagstone goes the crystal. Keep the effigy of power nearby to support you.

2. As you place the objects, recite the runes, creating a sacred vibrational field that resonates with the currency.

3. Ring the bell. Together, all elements of the spell create their own frequency that is more intense because they are adding to each other. As the vibrational current grows, an opening in the field of reality is created. You are able to see it clearly through the hagstone, which is symbolic of the metaphysical aperture that you are creating. And as the opening occurs, you discover that you are able to manipulate the aperture and make enough room for all your needs to flow freely to you.

# AMPLIFYING THE POWER

One way to amplify the power of your rune cast is by using a *galdr*. A *galdr* is a magick song in which the runes are sung. Giving voice to something amplifies it in many ways. It creates a vibrational link between the witch and the rune. It is also a way to engage with the space-time continuum because you can affect outcomes by aligning vibrational energy with the results you seek to manifest. Bringing a practice from the far distant past and reinterpreting it for modern use is a form of reconstruction.

Using a *galdr* is also an invocation. Invoking powers to come to your aid, no matter what your goal, will increase the energy and improve the outcome. Historically, a *galdr* was used to affect the outcome of a battle. Also referred to as a "shield song," a *galdr* was meant to be amplified. It is a sound intended to carry, whether to inspire or intimidate, bind or defeat.

A *galdr* was sung at a very high pitch and loud volume. The volume was increased by the positioning of shields over the mouth to create a resonance as the sound waves bounced off the surface of the metal. Holding your hands together, slightly cupped and about 2 or

3 inches away from your mouth, will also create a resonating chamber. It will direct the sound back to your own ears, and its power may be surprising at first. This is an excellent technique to use in coven craft as well, because even those witches who might be hesitant to engage with their own power in front of others can benefit from the modesty that covering the mouth allows.

In addition to shifting the energy of conflict into victory, a *galdr* was also used as part of the healing arts.

A *galdr* is rooted in runes, the meaning of which represent a wide expanse of energies and outcomes for myriad life events. A *galdr* could be chanted repeatedly near the bedside of a person who was afflicted or who had sustained an injury. It was even used to curse. Beyond victory, healing, and revenge, a *galdr* was used to summon supernatural spirits who could bring knowledge of the future, further connecting the purpose of runes as a system of divination.

To re-create the ancient energy of a *galdr* for modern use, choose a rune from your cast or choose one with intention that is aligned with the outcome that you seek. Use the hand-cupping method or use your charger from your altar (if you have one) and hold it in front of your nose and mouth. Face your altar and close your eyes. Envision the best possible outcome for everyone involved and sing your rune with as much power as you can muster. The song does not have to be pretty. It is not a performance. It can be primal or guttural or transcendent—whatever your spirit needs in that moment. You may find it wavers from a cry to a shriek or a cackle. There is no wrong way to sing a *galdr* as long as you put your heart and soul into it and make certain that the sound is loud and clear.

# *Chapter 10*

# RUNES OF STRENGTH AND PROTECTION

The mere sight of runes can inspire awe. They may also strike a chord of fear. For this reason, runes were frequently used in instruments of battle. Runes were emblazoned on shields, helmets, blades, and hilts. The sense of awe that they invoke would aid the warrior in battle with both power and protection.

A person experiences fear when they are confronted with things beyond their control. Anything that is unfamiliar or unknown can create a state of discomfort in the observer. This unsettling effect can be used to the advantage of the rune bearer. Victory means that while one will triumph, another will fall. In accordance with Newton's third law of motion, for every action there is an equal and opposite reaction. Any blow is absorbed by its target and changed by it. Keeping this principle in mind can give you an understanding of the impacts of magick. Even seeing a runic symbol has an effect on the observer, and anything that moves energy in your favor is worthy of magickal exploration.

# RUNE SIGILS FOR VICTORY: THE HELM OF AWE

Known as the Aegishjalmr, this spiked, rayed motif is said to carry with it the power of invincibility and was used in the Northern Tradition, which gives us the Norse runes. There is a spell in Icelandic folklore that helps a magick practitioner create the Aegishjalmr from lead (which we now know to be poisonous and do not recommend applying to skin for any purpose) and press it into their forehead while reciting the action taking place: "I bear the Helm of Awe between my brows." Doing so conferred unconquerability upon the bearer of the helm.

In deconstructing the Aegishjalmr, the name can be broken down into two parts. The first, "aegis," is the word for shield in Old Norse. Today, the word is used synonymously with protection. The aegis is a powerful symbol that transcends culture and time. Classical Greek Goddesses such as Athena were strongly associated with the shield, which in Athena's case was usually emblazoned with the head of the Gorgon. In *The Poetic Edda*, the dragon Fafnir steals the Aegishjalmr and attributes his invincibility to its efficacy. This association with the serpent energy of mythological creatures adds to the modern understanding of the Aegishjalmr's ability to strike fear in the hearts of those who encounter it. The latter part of the word, "hjalmr," translates to "helm" and is the etymological root of the word "helmet."

Some interpreters of myth claim that this translation meant that the Aegishjalmr was an actual physical helmet instead of a magickal sigil, but since the form of the Aegishjalmr was never definably fixed, it follows to reason that its definition is similarly fluid. "Helm" and "helmet" are not interchangeable words, however. To be at the helm of something is to be in a position of responsibility and authority and to be highly visible. It refers to the state of being out front or up front. This can be interpreted to mean leadership, fearlessness, or any number of strong qualities that would bring about victory and success in any endeavor. Some modern applications where the Aegishjalmr would be beneficial include:

- Confrontations
- Negotiations
- Court proceedings
- Online interactions

- Issues with coworkers or superiors
- Issues in relationships where there is a power differential, such as doctor/patient, teacher/student, or manager/employee

Keeping the Aegishjalmr at the top of your mind by tracing it on your forehead will remind you of your own invincibility. It can also help to lessen the power of your opposing force. Once you have traced the symbol on your forehead, visualize radiating vanquishing power that emanates from the center of the star, gains power as it travels down the staves, and pushes outward in any direction, as far as you need it to go and with as much force as you need it to have.

Since the form of the Aegishjalmr is not fixed, you can adapt it to your needs as long as your intention remains consistent and focused. The motifs and arrangements that the Aegishjalmr always have are:

- A central circle
- Eight rays beginning in the center and extending beyond the central circle
- Runes commonly believed to be Elhaz and Isa. The purpose of Isa is to "freeze" the enemy and render them incapable of an attack. Elhaz is heavily associated with protection, and its repeated presence confers multiple layers of protection that can be named by its bearer.

Modern iterations of the Aegishjalmr often include a circle of runes surrounding the rayed star motif, but these outer circles have not been authenticated. Although this symbol has nothing to do with Wicca, it bears a striking resemblance to the Wheel of the Year. The repetition of patterns and motifs is a unifying element among multiple cosmologies, and common threads are not atypical even though this does not prove they possess any common historical links.

## APOTROPAIC RUNES

Like the Vegvísir, the Aegishjalmr provides not only strength but also protection. Two elements these powerful symbols have in common are repeating staves and star motifs centered around a common intersecting point. You can modernize the elements of these powerful symbols by employing their common features and incorporating them into your personal needs and requests.

For example, if you feel that you require a ward against disease, you can take the Norse rune Sowilo and repeat it around a central circle. The resulting sigil becomes a pictographic representation of the sun and signifies the light and growth, fulfillment, vitality, and life force that this rune is associated with. Employing repetition and a circle motif is a powerful way to amplify the power of runes.

You may wish to use bindrunes, as is frequently seen in the various renderings of the Aegishjalmr. For example, if you are in need of victory no matter the situation, use the stave of Nauthiz and combine it with the apex of Teiwaz, repeating the idea that you are in need of victory.

# CREATING RUNE STAVES

Repeating rune staves around a central motif takes a little practice. Four-way and eight-rayed motifs are the easiest to start with because their spacing is simple to determine. You can personalize your sigil by determining the number of staves that will have particular meaning to you. For example, you can add up the numbers in your birth date: the day, the month, the year, and even the time. Keep adding until you arrive at the sum. Then, continue adding the numbers in the sum together until you get to a single number that is less than ten. This will determine the number of staves in your apotropaic, or protection, symbol. You can begin practicing the rough outline using a circle template, which will help you locate the center point of a circle and the vertical and horizontal half circle points, which you can outline with the aid of a straightedge and then mark equal divisions on depending on the final number of staves you plan to use.

Once you know the number of staves you will be working with, you will have to decide which rune system you are going to use. You can even use a synthesis of multiple systems if you like, but it is recommended to stick with just one. There is power in repetition, so each stave should have the same rune or bindrune. The choice of individual runes or bindrunes will be determined by your specific needs and purposes.

Practice drawing a single stave and then see if you can evenly repeat the pattern along the staves of the ray and circle motif that you sketched out using the circle template and straightedge. You may find that certain bindrunes do not lend themselves easily to the repeated pattern, and you may need to adjust the spacing. Keep experimenting until you are able to create your own personal sigil of protective, victorious magick.

## USING RUNE STICKS

In 1954, close to the southernmost point of Greenland, a startling archaeological discovery was made. Among the remains of textiles, fragments of bone, and tools and weapons fashioned from caribou antlers was a long pine stick carved with runes. Known as the Narsaq stick, this length of pine was covered in Norse runes, which had previously never been seen in Greenland. This was the first discovery of a Norse settlement in Greenland.

A total of four rune sticks were discovered and bore the marking of the Futhark in short twig form. It is believed that these sticks were carved by different people but that their use was probably the same: magick and cipher. One interpretation argues that one of the rune sticks is inscribed with a prayer for a safe passage at sea while another appears to contain some kind of riddle or cipher.

In addition to Norse runes, Ogham runes are often carved on sticks. You can carve or draw an intention on a stick and carry it with you or wear it on your person as a talisman or charm. You can incorporate a rune stick as part of a spell jar or larger magickal working. You can also use rune sticks in a similar way to Witch runes, enlivening them with friction by rolling them back and forth between your hands and then allowing them to fall and examining their position and relationship to each other. Take note of which runes face you, which runes are close, which are distant, and which rune sticks are touching to guide your interpretation.

# ACCEPTING OUTCOMES

Divination is an art. Many times, a practitioner will inadvertently reveal something they would have rather not known. Anytime a predictive endeavor is undertaken, there is some level of risk to the status quo. Remember that when predicting the future or foreseeing outcomes, all participants have free agency and personal will. A bad omen does not equate with a bad outcome. Take heed of signs and portents and move accordingly. A well-timed warning can be just the impetus needed to ward off a larger disaster. A short-term sacrifice will often be necessary, and ordeals are native to rune work.

Accepting the wide range of human experience can make you a more compassionate person, a more ethical person, and a more open and honest person. Yes, there is a danger in openness, but runes are also linked to protective magick. Knowledge and ability of the multiple applications of runes can leave a magick practitioner feeling empowered instead of vulnerable. And accepting an undesirable outcome is not the same as invoking it. It is always possible to avoid sailing directly into the storm if you have the courage to take the helm and direct your journey via a safer passage.

# Chapter 11

# LIGHTS AND SHADOWS: INCORPORATING RUNES IN CANDLE MAGICK AND MATRICES

Runes provide illumination. They allow us to examine aspects of our lives from many different perspectives. Runes will reveal information about the past and also describe what is coming into being. Because runes are tools of illumination, they are easily adapted to candle magick. Candle magick can incorporate runes in a variety of methods, including scribing and creating illuminated matrices. Incorporating runes into candle magick allows you to use a wide range of materials that are easy to obtain, such as tea lights, pillar candles, and taper candles. Using runes in candle magick will allow you to focus your intentions, enhance your meditations, and add power to your spellwork. A matrix is a specific type of altar arrangement that incorporates your runes, candles, and also your own sacred objects such as crystals and gemstones. The arrangement of a matrix is done to provide a visual focal point of your meditation as well as a method of creative expression.

The activities and exercises in this chapter can be used with any of the rune systems described in the previous chapters and can be adapted for different kinds of magickal workings, whether you wish to bring about a desired outcome, effect some sort of change in life, or simply augment the energy of your seasonal rituals or lunar observances.

## PILLAR CANDLE CARVING BASICS

Pillar candles are a staple of witchcraft. They are used for spells, charms, and rituals as well as for ambience. Pillar candles come in a variety of diameters and heights and are large enough to carve into.

Carving a candle is a magickal act. It forces the practitioner to plan and focus. With candle carving, there is no erasing, so everything must be done with intention. This in itself is a potent exercise in developing your psychic abilities. Pillar candles are particularly useful in rune work because of the large surface area. This allows for creating a sequence, recording and illuminating a rune cast, and empowering your magickal practice.

## THE SCRIBE

Before considering what to carve, consider which tool you want to carve with. In witchcraft, there are several different types of tools dedicated to magickal work. The runes are one such tool: They are used to tap into mysteries and spiritual knowledge. Runes, usually carved in stone, can also be carved into candles. Most witches use a bolline (which is the "practical" blade or "white-handled knife," as opposed to the athame, which is the double-edged blade often with a black handle, used for carving out sacred space) for candle carving, when using runes in candle magick. Using the bolline is important because the choice of implement will have some effect or impact on the spell at hand.

In magick, many things are taken into account, including color, phase of the moon, time of year, and even the time of day. Each auspicious element that is carefully chosen with clear intentions will amplify the outcome either by hastening it or by adding to its effectiveness. This effectiveness is what is referred to as "power" in witchcraft. It is not to suggest that one person does or should hold power over another person, or that a person possesses power as a characteristic of themselves. Power is ascribed to the effectiveness of the work. The spell was either effective or it wasn't. Generally, the more successful or effective spells are the ones in which the most work was placed.

If you want powerful results, you must empower each act with intention. A powerful witch is not one who subjugates the will of others to their own; it is the witch who is able to channel intention into manifestation. Choosing tools with care is a key element to successful manifestation. In time, you may find that your witchcraft is so strong that tools become less important, but until then, honing your focus on intention and calling desirable outcomes into being is a worthy undertaking.

Since runes are often carved, think about the nature of the work at hand when choosing a scribe. The scribe can be dedicated and chosen for a specific spell or magickal working. For example, you would choose a different tool for an uncrossing candle than you would for a hearth blessing candle. Think first in broad terms, such as invoking, banishing, or changing. You can get more specific from there, but broad strokes will lead you to the correct materials for the task at hand: either carving runes to augment a candle spell or inscribing a favorable rune cast upon a candle in order to intensify or hasten the predicted outcome.

## Making a Scribe

A scribe can be a dedicated magickal tool or an ordinary household item. A sharpened chopstick or a hefty toothpick or skewer would make a serviceable scribe. A pin or a tack would make a serviceable scribe as well. The more energy you put into your candle rune craft, the more you get out of it. There is a direct relationship between energy you invest in a rune cast and a candle carving and the amount of energy returned to you. It is a cycle of energy released and replenished. This tenet of magick is as true as the air we breathe. Just as we create a change in the composition of our surrounding atmosphere with every breath, so too are we able to effect change by focusing with magick intention.

It doesn't take much to create your own scribe. All you need is a pencil sharpener and a slender twig about the same diameter as your pinkie finger and about as long as the base of your palm to the tip of your little finger. Take the twig and sharpen it just as you would a pencil, and you have a ready-made rune scribe. You can also cut it using kitchen scissors or pruning scissors to make a diagonal cut. The type of wood you choose depends on the nature of the work at hand. For example:

- **Oak:** If your rune cast was favorable or otherwise memorable or particularly revealing, using an oak scribe will increase its power.
- **Apple:** If your query or cast was about love or relationships, use an apple wood scribe.
- **Willow:** To assuage grief, use willow.
- **Yew:** To memorialize a person or honor the dead, use yew.

Letter openers can make serviceable scribes, but take note of any designs or words they might have engraved on them and judge if this will have an impact on your work. Additionally, letter openers are not ergonomic. When using a scribe, you want control, which means you will be holding it close to the point. This can make the letter opener less than ideal.

If you are seeking to evoke or acknowledge a radical change, take a meditative forest walk and look for a fallen tree. Examine the breaking point, where the forces of nature and gravity toppled one of the most resilient living things on earth. When you look at the breaking point, you are engaging with a point of radical change. If there are paradigms you need to tear down, if you are truly ready to break free of old patterns and topple the past, you may find the perfect scribe for your work is revealed in the breaking point.

If your focus is ancestral work or honoring the dead, look for an uprooted tree and trim off a sturdy root. Roots are an important part of the underground communication system of trees, and roots symbolize ties to family and to the land. If you are occupying stolen land, as many people are, you may want to use a root scribe to honor the indigenous spirits of the land on which you live.

### Railroad Spike

You can also use a railroad spike as a scribe. Many witches already have railroad spikes, but if you don't, they are very easy to obtain. A railroad spike makes an excellent scribe for scribing pillar and taper candles. Made of iron or steel and relatively inexpensive, railroad spikes are commonly used in protective magick particularly of the home.

## The Template

Now that you have your scribe, the next things you will need are a piece of paper, a ruler, scissors, a calculator, a pencil, and a pin. Pillar candles come in many diameters. You will need to know the diameter of the candle. If you do not know the diameter, use the ruler to measure from one side to the other, and then take note of that measurement and multiply it by 3.14 to get the circumference. Once you have the circumference of the candle, cut a strip of paper about an inch wide and the same length as the circumference. Next, divide the length of the strip of paper by the number of runes you used in your rune cast. For example, if you did a five-rune spread and are using a 3-inch-diameter pillar candle, you would divide 9.42 by 5 in order to get 1.88 inches. You should have a strip of paper about an inch wide and a little less than 9.5 inches long. Using the ruler, draw a vertical line every 1.88 inches on the strip of paper. Feel free to round up and use 2-inch markers. The template does not need to be entirely precise, but if you follow the formula, it will come out perfectly.

In between each 2-inch delineation, draw the runes from your five-rune cast on the paper strip from right to left. Then tape the strip of paper around the candle, either at the top, middle, or bottom, depending on how quickly you want the cast to manifest. Some runes will be celebrations, and you will want them to last longer. These go at center or below center. Sometimes, timing is of the essence and you want to get on with things. In that case, wrap the strip of paper around the top.

Once you've secured the 1-inch strip of paper with the runes drawn on it around the appropriate place on your candle, using the pin, press through a few points along the runes so that once the paper is removed, you will be able to recognize them and follow the pattern. When you have made pinpricks through all of the characters all around the diameter of the candle, remove the paper. Then, using your scribe, connect the dots to score the rune pattern into the candle. As you scribe, focus on the prophecy revealed in the rune cast. Think about what it is that you want to accelerate or prolong, celebrate or change. You can scribe over the rune staves several times so that they are consistent and deep. Next, you will dress the candle.

# Dressing the Runes

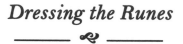

Once your candle is carved, you are ready for the final step, which is to dress the candle. Dressing the candle is a form of consecration and cements your spell as a magickal act.

## You Will Need

- Aromatic resin, chosen to augment the spell, such as copal for love, frankincense for reverence, or patchouli for grounding
- Mortar and pestle
- Candle carved with runes
- Essential oil blend that is suited to the spell or magickal working at hand

## Directions

1. Put the resin into your mortar and pestle and crush it into a fine powder.

2. Apply the powder directly into the candle carvings.

3. Apply a few drops of the oil to the candle on the opposite side of the carving. As you apply the oil, speak your intention and recite the runes as you trace around them. This will help activate and amplify their power. Make sure to avoid rubbing oil directly into the scribed runes.

4. After the oil is applied, lightly brush off any remaining powdered resin. The oil will consecrate the candle for spellwork, and the resin will make the runes more noticeable.

5. Now you are ready to light your candle and enjoy the successful outcome that you have brought into being.

# JAR CANDLES

Pillar candles often come in jars, but the most desirable jar candles for witches are those that can be removed from their jars. Since removable jar candles are not always in convenient supply, you may want to adapt your runic candle magick to candles that are poured directly into their jar.

You can focus on a rune spread and use it in an altar dedication by affixing your runestones or tiles directly to the outside of the glass jar using poster tacking putty, available at most office supply stores. Pinch off a pea-sized amount of putty and adhere it to the back of your runestone so that the character is facing outward, then stick the rune onto the jar. The poster tack is removable and reusable, and it will not damage your runes. This way, you can keep your rune spread illuminated as you integrate its message and teaching.

# TAPER CANDLES

Bindrunes are easily adaptable to carving into tapered candles. First, practice creating bindrunes on a piece of paper. Draw a straight line down the middle and choose the runes you wish to combine with intention and care. Think about if you are trying to evoke a particular sound, such as the name of the desire you wish to call into being, or if you are more interested in a series of metaphysical changes. Is your intention literal? If you can name exactly what you want, then use a transliteration, substituting runes in place of the letters that you would use to spell out your desire in your own mother tongue. If you cannot specifically name your desire, but you know you need something to move or change, then use that as the basis for your intention. Instead of consulting the phonetic chart or alphabetic equivalents, you will need to consult with the meanings of the runes.

On a sheet of paper, measure and mark a box that is a similar measurement to the length and width of the candle you wish to carve. Draw a vertical line down the center of the box. Then choose your runes individually. Start with no more than two or three to create a basic rune stave. They can be initials, or desired influences in a sequence. Put the runes on top of the vertical line and see where they share common staves. How you arrange them is up to you. You might wish to align them sequentially from top to bottom, or you may wish to put the most important one in the center, the one that represents you or your desired outcome, and then place one above and one below to imply an alignment with celestial (above) and earth (below) energies. When you have found the common lines along the stave, move the runes aside and draw them directly on the center line. This will become your template for carving a bindrune.

Once you've drawn your bindrune on the paper, attach the paper lengthwise to the candle and tape it to hold it in place. Using a pin, pierce through the paper to make a pattern of the bindrune on the wax. Then remove the paper and carve the bindrune into the candle with your scribe. Some suggestions (depending on the nature of your spell) for your bindrune are:

- Your initials
- The initials of someone you love
- The initials of someone in need of healing
- Your name
- Your magickal name
- The name of a place you want to live
- The class you need to pass
- The outcome that you want

Once your bindrune has been carved, dress the candle with powdered resin and oil. This is an act of consecration, and it will also make the bindrune more visible. If possible, allow your candle to burn down uninterrupted.

## Using Tea Lights to Illuminate Runes

Tea lights are affordable and easy to obtain. They are similar to votive candles but shorter and come in their own small metal containers. Tea lights also burn down in a few hours, which is plenty of time for a deep meditation on your intention. You can create an illuminated rune as a meditation, to amplify a spell, or to shed light on a situation. The rune you choose to illuminate will come from the first rune from a recent cast. This is the rune that most often represents your present state of mind in relation to the situation surrounding your query. The oracle is pointing you to examine this aspect of yourself in order to get you centered and prepared for the predictions that are soon to unfold. A rune created from an array of tea lights is beautiful to behold. This process literally sheds light on your present circumstance. If you are part of a practicing coven that creates a supportive environment, the illuminated rune can be a powerful focal point on an altar or for the center of a circle.

## You Will Need

- Full sheet of grid paper
- 24 tea light candles, or more, depending on how big you want your illumination to be
- Pencil or pen
- Scissors
- Large serving tray or flat surface

## Directions

1. Use the first rune from your cast and draw it on the grid paper, taking up as much of the paper as possible.

2. Take the tea lights and arrange them on the paper so that they are covering the rune character that you have drawn. With the pencil or pen, trace around the bottoms of the tea lights. You may have to move them in and out of place in order to get a good circle.

3. When your drawing has been covered in circles, fold the paper in half along the midpoint of the circles in order to cut them out easily. You will have to make multidirectional folds in order to be precise.

4. Unfold the paper and smooth it out so that it lies flat. Place it on the tray or on top of your altar (you may wish to consider putting something like a trivet in between the tray and your altar so that the surface of your altar does not get too hot) and set the tea lights in each open circle.

5. Lift the paper and set it aside. Light your candles and you will have an illuminated rune made from an array of candles. You can use the flames as a focal point for your meditation as you focus on bringing your desired outcome into being.

# CREATING A RUNE MATRIX

Many practicing witches have a cupboard or cabinet full of ingredients, tools, and objects that help them focus their magick and enhance their practice. These include herbs, candles, crystals, oracles, and effigies. These are used in altar craft, spellcasting, and the creation of charms. For advanced altar craft, creating crystal matrices is a powerful way to enhance a spell by creating a link among the practitioner, the intention, and the metaphysical properties of different minerals and crystals. It is possible to use runes in a similar way by creating a matrix using rune sticks or tiles, candles, and crystals. Building a rune matrix puts a lot of control in the hands of the practitioner. It is a different way to use runes as a part of witchcraft that does not involve consulting the oracle.

To create a rune matrix, you will need to use rune sticks or tiles, which you can purchase or make yourself. Ogham runes are often carved on sticks due to their association with particular trees. You will also need six votive candles in glass jars. Choose the colors of the candles with care, because the matrix that you create should be part of a goal. The matrix itself is not the goal. It is more of a practice to further develop your spellcraft. A rune matrix can be quite beautiful and decorative, but there is a deeper meaning behind it. If you are unsure which candle colors you should be working with, you can consult the following table for some general color associations.

| Color Relationship Correspondences | |
| --- | --- |
| **Color** | **Association** |
| White | Moon, reflected wisdom, inclusiveness, transformation, constant change, beginnings, protection, peace |
| Black | Sign of Capricorn, scrying, mystery, conquest, reflection, crossing and uncrossing, reversals |
| Red | Sign of Aries and Scorpio, initiative, passion, survival, creativity, ambition |

| Color Relationship Correspondences | |
|---|---|
| **Color** | **Association** |
| Orange | Sign of Leo, heightened activity, strength, success after difficulty, divinity, illumination |
| Yellow | Sign of Taurus and Libra, wisdom, intellect, scholarship, strong will, illumination, love, persistence, spiritual awakening |
| Green | Sign of Cancer and Virgo, the heart, matters of love, life, rebirth, spiritual growth, wealth |
| Blue | Sign of Sagittarius, Aquarius, and Pisces, idealism, potential, communication, wholeness |
| Purple | Sign of Gemini, attainment, duality, transmutation, transformations, spiritual fire, spiritual quest |

Start in the center of your altar and place one of the candles there. Then select five runes and arrange them around the outside perimeter of the candle so that they are evenly spaced. Place another candle at the other end of each rune stick or tile. You will choose which runes to use based on your intention. Consult the lists of meanings in order to make your choice. You may wish to focus on a single influence or many. For example, you might select a combination of runes that you would want to see in your ideal cast. When you have selected your runes and placed them accordingly, you can add to your matrix by placing tumbled stones or crystals in the negative spaces in between the rune sticks and the candles.

When choosing which stones to work with, consider their metaphysical properties. You can consult any number of resources for information on the associations and meanings of a variety of gems and minerals, or you can choose on instinct based on what you find visually or energetically appealing.

# LINES, CROSSES, AND CURVES

As you become more adept at creating matrices using rune sticks, runestones, or tiles along with candles and crystals, you may find that you wish to create more complex patterns. Patterns occur in nature and are imbued with natural magick. The divine order of the universe follows numerous patterns that can be readily observed in all life forms from plants, to sea creatures, to the planets and stars. Developing your skill at creating a matrix aligns your practice with all energies both terrestrial and celestial.

As you arrange your matrix, you will find that it is a creative outlet, a place where you can focus, and something that beautifies your surroundings. Incorporate new patterns by adding intersecting lines, exploring the places where two lines meet. A cross in a matrix can represent a crossroads to help in decision-making or it can signify a celebration, such as a point of change in the Wheel of the Year. If you continue to add vertical, diagonal, and horizontal crosses, you will make a star motif like the one in the Witch runes. (There has long been speculation that the origin of the word "witch" is connected to "wicce," which is believed by many to have an etymological connection to Wicca and means "to bend" or "to change.") You can also add curved lines to indicate accepting the winds of change when they blow through your life, to imitate the spirals found in nature, or just to remind yourself to smile. Whether your practice is secular or spiritual, learning the variations in matrix work will lead you to a deeper understanding of how magick works and how every color, pattern, shape, intention, and action shapes our reality.

In magick, accepted realities include nature and the observable world, human-made creations and the manipulation of the natural world, and entities and experiences that are unseen but deeply felt (including communication with oracles and spirits), as well as personal gnosis, which is spiritual knowledge that is gained by an individual practitioner but that does not necessarily have an external validation attached to it. Subtle changes in the environment, both observable and unseen but intuitively felt, during a magickal working are accepted as an affirmation that the work has power. One theme that solidly recurs in all forms of magick is change.

### Lines

Beginning from a central point in your matrix and adding lines that radiate outward is a symbolic way to manifest. You will make it symbolically real on the earthly plane by infusing it with light, earth magick, and rune magick from the astral plane until it becomes your actual reality. A single line can represent your present path, and repeating this pattern can amplify your intention so that the energy is moving in all directions. For example, a center candle or crystal can be surrounded by five runes. Five is a sacred number in the divine order of the universe. Every fruit comes from a flower with five petals. Cut open an apple and you will see five seeds arranged in the same way. Five aspects of a worldly desire can be articulated. These could represent the pathway to your desired outcome: health, abundance, comfort, love, and peace.

## THE UNSEEN RUNE

It is common for many modern sets of runes to include a blank rune. A blank rune is the same material, size, and shape as the other runes in the set, but it will not have an inscription of any kind. As its name implies, the blank rune is devoid of a character; there is nothing on it. If you decide to create your own rune set, you may wish to consider including a blank rune as well. The blank rune is non-existent in the ancient script. A blank rune is historically inconsistent with the origin and purpose of runes. But while the blank rune is a modern construct, its presence is no less important.

Imagine if your life were a blank slate. What if you were free of expectation and released from obligation? What would you create if necessity were no longer your guide? The blank rune gives the witch permission to dream, to create themselves anew. The blank rune represents the ultimate mystery, the unwritten word, the unseen hand, and the unknowable essence of all things esoteric. It can be perceived as neutral, having no intrinsic value judgment of favorable or unfavorable, good or ill. It bears a certain similarity to the wheel of fate with a "what will be, will be" energy surrounding it. The unseen rune also allows us to acknowledge our limitations and calls us to pay attention to the things that have escaped our scrutiny. The unseen rune may be a call to peer deeper and try harder.

Desirable states of being such as tranquility and peace can be reflected in the unseen rune, as there is nothing there to contradict or suggest otherwise. Engaging with the unseen can also mean exploring forgotten pathways in addition to the unknown. The blank rune can be seen as an opportunity to define yourself anew or to reclaim a former identity. This can be particularly helpful during times of great transition. Whether the change is internal, external, or both, think of the blank rune as a fresh page upon which to write the trajectory that you are on the verge of launching into. Lacking symbol and sound, the blank rune projects nothing and reflects everything.

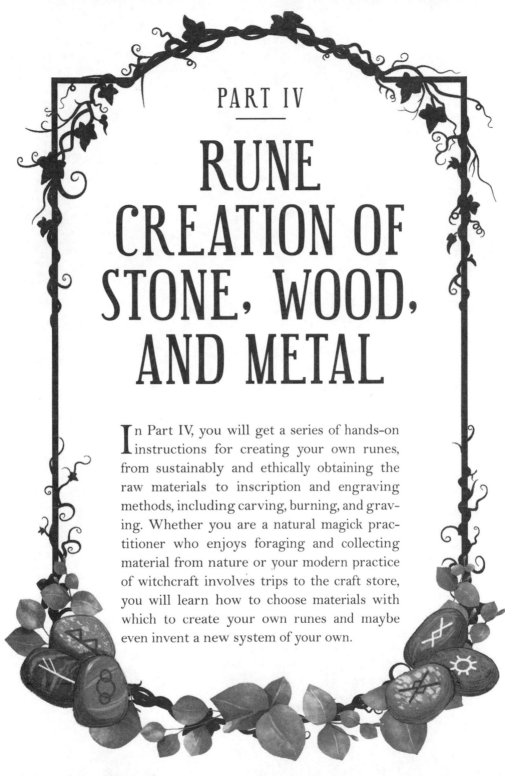

# PART IV

## RUNE CREATION OF STONE, WOOD, AND METAL

In Part IV, you will get a series of hands-on instructions for creating your own runes, from sustainably and ethically obtaining the raw materials to inscription and engraving methods, including carving, burning, and graving. Whether you are a natural magick practitioner who enjoys foraging and collecting material from nature or your modern practice of witchcraft involves trips to the craft store, you will learn how to choose materials with which to create your own runes and maybe even invent a new system of your own.

# Chapter 12

# THE PHYSICAL RUNES

Know how to cut them, know how to read them,
Know how to stain them, know how to prove them,
Know how to evoke them, know how to score them

—*The Poetic Edda*, translated by Taylor and Auden

Runes are physical entities that have been imbued with spiritual powers. We experience them not only through sight, sound, and touch but also through our psychic senses. Since we are all earthly beings, having a deep understanding of the physical nature of runes is important to understanding them and using them on higher levels.

Because so many ancient runic writings appear non-lexical and defy interpretation, one can surmise that a certain amount of their indecipherable nature was intentional. Runic writings were often understood only by their creators, and the artifacts reveal that there is historically no right or wrong way to use runes. Transferring this idea into the modern world, there is no right or wrong way to create a set of runes. Whether they are burned in wood or carved in stone, creating a set of runes by hand does not require much outside of rudimentary tools that many households already possess. In this chapter, we will explore different methods of rune creating, informed by history and both feasible and relevant today.

# CHOOSING YOUR MEDIUM

Traditionally made of natural materials, runes lend themselves to a wide variety of methods and substances. In order to choose the medium from which you will create your runes, there are several factors that must play into your decision. A set of handmade runes is highly personal and very magickal. The materials you choose should reflect your own ethos and the manner in which you engage with witchcraft as a whole. For example, you may choose to use recycled or upcycled materials. Your materials can be cost-effective and yet still beautiful. Think about repurposing and reusing rigid packing materials such as decorative cardboard boxes. Perhaps you identify with Druidic bards and wish to use wood that you cut or gather yourself. Maybe you use crystals frequently and are ready to try some basic lapidary. If you are vegan or vegetarian, you probably reject the idea of using shell or bone in your creation.

Before choosing your medium, ask yourself, "What kind of witch am I?" and see what kind of material the answer will lead you to. You also want to consider your current skill set and what your artistic and craft capabilities are. Here are some recommendations along with the rationales behind why certain materials will resonate with your practice more than others. This is not meant to be a comprehensive list, but a general set of identities that modern witches use to describe their paths.

### *Traditional/Initiatory Witch*

If your practice is Alexandrian, Gardnerian, or British Traditional Witchcraft, which are different types of Wicca, you will have a high priestess who can guide you toward what is specific to your coven. You may also look to a deity to inspire your choice. For example, if you are dedicated to Isis, you may want to select handfuls of tumbled turquoise. Turquoise is relatively soft, easy to carve, and bears a similar color and appearance to Egyptian faience. Faience is a type of sintered glass made by adding color while applying heat, so you can even choose flat glass marbles and paint the staves on them.

---

### Materials and Methods

In earlier chapters, you learned about different kinds of rune casts. Remember that when you choose a material to create your own runes, it will have an impact on the types of rune casts you are able to do. Don't throw glass runes! They can chip and break and become dangerous. You might find that there is a relationship between the material and the method. Sticks and bones are easily thrown, but glass and rocks can hurt you.

---

## Eclectic Witch

Eclectic witches borrow from multiple cultures and traditions, which makes material selection very easy. Ceramic clay, air-dried clay, wood, metal, or stone would be appropriate for the eclectic witch, depending on with which aspect of oracle they seek to engage. For example, an eclectic witch who uses a mix of Classical Greco-Roman and Celtic deities in their practice might choose fired clay in order to pay homage to the artifacts of Greek pottery and the ancient Celtic fire festivals. Renting space at a pottery studio and getting your hands in the clay that makes them would be a rewarding experience.

## Hedge Witch

Hedge witches are known for exploring liminal spaces. Unusual materials or found objects would be appealing to the hedge witch. Finding the magick in everyday items and making them sacred, such as buttons or coins or keys, would be something for the hedge witch to consider.

## Kitchen Witch

The kitchen witch is adept with herbs and fire. Using culinary ingredients and burning would suit the kitchen witch. Imagine a set of handmade runes with staves burned onto whole nutmeg or cinnamon sticks. This would produce an aromatic and magickal set of runes. The kitchen witch may find themselves slashing runes across the tops of rising loaves of bread and using pyromancy as a part of their rune path.

### Sea Witch

The sea witch will be attuned to runes painted on sea glass or shells or carved in stones found near the water's edge. Also, reclaimed driftwood would make a powerful material on which to base a set of runes. Runes were used heavily in seafaring to invoke a safe passage, bless a journey, and protect against storms at sea. Clear or semi-opaque materials will be attractive to the sea witch. Attuned with oceans, lakes, and seas, the sea witch has an aptitude for influencing the weather and may find Elder Futhark and Witch runes to be a natural fit for their divination path.

### Green Witch

The green witch is the steward of the earth. Recycled and upcycled materials such as repurposed or reclaimed wood make an energetic alignment between the practitioner and the tool. The green witch may also like to use air-dried clay, which would make for an ephemeral and easy-to-recycle set of runes. Green witches are adept at folk magick and may gravitate toward rustic materials and a rune path that is grounded in the earth, such as runes burned on slices of a broom handle and practicing casts out of doors in a grove of trees.

### Hereditary Witch

The hereditary witch may have a set of runes in the family or may be instructed in ancestral magick. Ask the family elders about the methods and materials relevant to the ancestral line and let family bonds be your guide. If this information is not accessible, it may be possible to divine it through trance meditation or past-life regression. All events, all things seen, are still being projected into the universe. A witch need only accelerate their vibrational frequencies to catch up with the past in order to understand it.

### Cosmic Witch

The cosmic witch is immersed in astrology, planetary alignments, knowledge of the zodiac, celestial events, divining, and interpreting horoscopes. Runes made from birthstones and minerals that are attuned to constellations will be particularly attractive to the cosmic witch.

*Part IV: Rune Creation of Stone, Wood, and Metal*

# How to Carve Runes in Stone

———— ✑ ————

You don't need to be a highly skilled lapidary in order to carve runes into stone. Most runes are simple in design and do not require a significant amount of expertise. The most important thing to remember is that the object used to carve must be harder than the material being carved. This is relatively easy to determine by consulting the Mohs' scale. This scale is a list of how hard certain minerals are in relation to others. At the top of the scale are diamond (the hardest substance known) and corundum (the mineral name for rubies and sapphires). Carbide steel is also capable of cutting through softer stones or ceramics. Choosing a carving tool that is coated in either diamond or corundum will enable you to carve on every other type of stone or mineral. While diamond and corundum may sound expensive, remember that not all minerals are gem-quality material, and there is plenty of industrial diamond and corundum that is used exclusively for toolmaking.

## You Will Need

- Selection of tumbled stones, relatively equal in size, preferably with smooth, flat surfaces—get a few more than you need so that you have at least one to practice on and another extra in case a stone chips or breaks or you need a do-over
- Shallow dish of water
- Straightedge, such as a small ruler
- French curve or circle template
- Fine-point permanent marker
- Safety goggles
- Hair tie, if needed
- Diamond or corundum carving burr, such as a round .010 millimeter (usually sold in packs of six or more)
- Rotary tool

# Directions

1. Set up your materials at a dedicated workspace, then sit with your stones and touch them. If they were purchased, place them in the water first, then take them out one by one and dry them.

2. Listen to them. Ask if they came from a river or from a pocket of heat and pressure deep within the earth. Allow space in your mind for the stones to give you their stories. They are as old as time itself. Think about how you acquired them. Did you pay a fair price? Did you take the time to make a careful consideration? Or did you collect them yourself, and do they sing you the song of your travels and adventures? Perhaps they were gathered near your home or property. Allow yourself to sync with the energy of the stones and invite them to tell you their origin.

3. Once the stones are dry, choose the rune system you want to use. Then, carefully using the straightedge or the French curve or circle template, begin drawing the runes onto the stones with the marker.

4. Once you have drawn all the runes, put on the safety goggles, and if you have long hair, make sure it is pulled back and secured. Using the carving burr, set the rotary tool on low speed and carve a few lines in your practice stone. If the stone becomes hot, you can dip it in the water to cool it, but be careful not to erase your character. Once you get confident, you can begin carving by moving the rotary tool back and forth along one part of the character until it is sufficiently deep and then move on to another part. Do not trace the character over the whole stone in one pass. Carve small parts at a time by going back and forth over the same segment of the line you wish to carve. Go slowly and check your work. Try holding the rotary tool in one place and moving the stone beneath it to cut the rune staves.

# FINISHING YOUR RUNES

Now it is time to focus on each rune individually. You have chosen a system, so be sure to have the names and meanings of your runes bookmarked in the previous chapters for easy reference. You can recite their names as you carve them, and pronounce them to charge each stone. You are essentially calling an entry point to the oracle into being. Do this with knowledge and respect. Think about their attributes, and if you weren't solid on your characters, names, and meanings, you will be by the end of this experience.

After your carving is done, you may want to paint the recessed areas to make the characters stand out and make them easier to read. You may wonder, "Why go to the trouble of carving?" Carving is consistent with the origins of runes. Even in reconstruction and reproduction, care is always taken to approximate authenticity whenever possible. Furthermore, if you keep your runes in a pouch, they will eventually show some wear and tear, as the stones can wear on each other, causing the paint to fade or flake off. Painting in the recessed areas of the carvings puts the paint below the surface of the stones so that it does not come into direct contact with other stones, making the application last longer. You can use a paint pen (any color) or craft paint with a very thin brush or toothpick to do the painting. Allow the paint to dry, and your runes are ready to be used.

## *Metal Runes*

Creating a set of metal runes is not as daunting as you may first think. Since runes have been emblazoned on helmets, swords, and shields, creating a set of runes in metal has a certain air of authenticity about it. This can be accomplished using tools you may already have in your house. If you do not, then most if not all can be readily obtained from a hardware store.

### You Will Need
- Tracing template of the desired silhouette shape, such as oval, round, or rectangular

- Malleable sheet metal, such as copper with a B&S Gauge of 20 (or 0.80 millimeter)
- Fine-point permanent marker
- Heavy scissors or shears
- Clear tape
- Wood or steel block
- Hammer
- Selection of two or three flathead screwdrivers in different sizes
- Sandpaper (200 grit) or file (#2 cut)

## Directions

1. Choose your desired template silhouette and, using the marker, begin tracing the outlines onto the sheet metal.

2. Draw the runes one by one in the center of each outline.

3. Using the heavy scissors or shears, cut out the silhouettes and tape them to the wood or steel block. You may find that the metal has warped a bit from the cutting, and you may need to tap the edges lightly with the hammer. The block is there to absorb the blow of the hammer.

4. Take a scrap piece of metal from the negative space of your cutouts and practice making the rune staves. Draw a few rune staves on the extra metal, then use a screwdriver to make indentations in the metal by holding it with one hand directly on top of the rune design that you have drawn and gently hitting the butt end of the screwdriver handle with the hammer. Experiment with how hard you will need to hit in order to make an impression that is deep enough to be visible but not so deep that it completely penetrates the sheet.

5. After you have practiced a bit and have the ability to achieve consistent results, take one of your metal cutouts and tape it to the wood or steel block. Line up a screwdriver with the staves of the rune and tap the butt end with the hammer, mimicking the technique you just practiced. Once it is hit, the metal will bend a bit. Remove it from the block and turn it over, then lightly tap on the back side to flatten it out.

6. Use the sandpaper or file to remove any rough or sharp edges. You will find that metal runes are quite durable and make a pleasant sound when mixed together.

# BURNING RUNES

You can burn runes into wood, using a wood-burning tool or a chemical pen. Both the Ogham runes and the Norse runes are heavily associated with trees, which makes wood an authentic choice for the basis of a rune reconstruction project. You can buy small wood slices at a craft store or you may wish to find a branch or bough of a specific type of tree, such as oak, and create your own wood slices.

Whichever material you choose, remember to avoid the taboo of burning a sacred tree, such as birch. Due to its dramatic white bark, birch can be ubiquitous in craft supply outlets, but because it is unmistakable, it is also easy to avoid. Birch might be an acceptable choice for runes but not with the burning method. If you are drawn to using birch wood for your rune set, mark the staves by carving or painting, but not by burning.

To burn runes onto wood, have a small fan pointed away from your workspace and plan your work in a well-ventilated area. Smoke can burn your eyes; pointing the fan away from you will draw the smoke away. A universal point, which resembles a chisel tip, will work well for Norse runes and Ogham runes. For Witch runes, you will need a point tip or a chemical wood-burning pen.

A chemical pen contains a liquid substance that produces a charred effect when a heat source is applied. You can use the chemical pen to go over your fine-point pen drawings of Witch runes and then go over the chemical pen markings with a lighter or candle. When you're using the chemical pen, it is important to smooth out the wood surface with sandpaper first. If the surface is too rough, you will not be able to apply the liquid evenly. The liquid chars very quickly, so the wood does not catch fire. The wood-burning chemical pen is fun and easy and can be adapted as part of a candle meditation, as you can work by candlelight and then hold each rune up to the flame, charging it and scribing it in the same action.

# PERSONALIZING YOUR RUNES

Personalizing runes is a type of dedication. By now, your runes may already be highly personal. For example, you decided on a system with which you have an affinity either through ancestry, travel, migration, or some other cultural connection. You have chosen a material that aligns with your chosen path, and you have taken action by picking up the tools and engaging in a gentle act of transformation where mundane objects are made magickal. You have considered storage and handling and made conscious and aware decisions about how your approach to runes impacts the level of communication and divination that you are able to achieve.

If you are using tiles or stones for your runes, then each rune will have two sides. On the reverse side of the character, you may wish to add your own personal symbology, such as your planetary sign, your zodiac sign, or a bindrune of your own initials—anything that will be in accord with the archaic use of runes for labeling and denoting ownership. Personalizing your runes can extend to how you store them as well. Your initial bindrune can be easily embroidered on the pouch you keep your runes in, or you could use decoupage on the exterior of the box by layering images and colors that you find pleasing and representative of your identity.

# PURCHASING A SET OF RUNES

There are any number of reasons why you may want to forgo the DIY path and just purchase a set of runes. Rune crafters run the gamut from independent individual artisans and magick workers who sell one-of-a-kind or limited numbers of sets of handmade runes to large chain companies.

Runes can be for sale and still made by hand with the intent that they will be used for magickal purposes. Runes are also sold as a curiosity and as a game. This does not preclude them from being dedicated to a magickal purpose. While it is preferable to be able to see and touch the runes in person before purchasing, this may not always be possible if you are dealing with an online seller. The reason for having the tactile experience before purchasing is because there are sellers who will describe their runes inaccurately, sometimes even claiming that glass is a semiprecious stone. Asking a direct question will not always result in a correct answer, as sellers may not even be aware of misrepresented materials. No matter what type of witch you are, it is highly likely that you have experience handling natural materials and can hopefully energetically distinguish between the cool density of stone and the tepid lightness of plastic.

# *Chapter 13*

# THE METAPHYSICAL RUNES

J ust as there is a place where two perpendicular roads meet, there is a place where the unseen meets perceivable reality. When Odin spied the runes, was he calling them into a perceivable reality because they were already in existence on another plane? Metaphysical philosophy supports this idea. While there is a separation between mind and matter, one is no less real than the other.

The mysteries of the universe are composed of unknowable depths. Lack of perception does not prove lack of existence. In the runes, we see the intersection of oracle, symbol, sound, and object. There is no doubt that runes are made of perceptible matter, but what of their mystical associations? These attributes of mystery and oracle are widely accepted to be intrinsic to runes. If they can be noticed, uncovered, discovered, or otherwise revealed either by a God, a Druid, or a witch, is any rune system less a part of reality? Accepting the existence of runes as a metaphysical transmission of communication that is part of reality will open up new channels for psychic growth.

# THOUGHT BEHIND RUNIC ALPHABETS

The desire to reach for things beyond our grasp, whether it is a distant land, a promise of treasure, or the chance for love, has been one of the driving forces behind the evolution of cultures. The human longing for *more* remains as palpable today as ever. Our society becomes more global and yet, ironically, we become more isolated, entranced by devices, limiting our interactions, moving further and further away from touch and voice and intimacy.

Even as we drift apart, immersing ourselves in wireless digital words, humans are still seeking connection. Followers. Likes. Reactions. People still have a deep desire to be seen and understood.

Once again, we see a rise in image-driven communication and pictographic literacy. The use of emojis bears some strong resemblances to hieroglyphs: minor alterations in an expression communicate a particular kind of emotion. Emojis can be personalized to resemble their sender. This modern practice is hardly different from the use of runes. Symbols are still used to show possession or honor, or lay claim. If you can customize an emoji sticker, why not conjure more unique symbols?

Like the runes of *The Poetic Edda*, anything that we can perceive on this plane of existence reveals itself in some way, and can be noticed, then shared. If the purpose of language is to communicate, and the purpose of alphabetic writing is to make meaning, and humanity has a persistent propensity for symbols of all varieties, then there is nothing to preclude the individual from creating a unique system upon which to build an original significance.

# CREATING YOUR OWN UNIQUE RUNES

As was previously stated, all linguistics and systems of language are created by people. And people have long sought to explain and elevate their own existence by likening themselves to Gods. Language evolved into literacy as spoken words became represented by lines, crosses, and curves. Early writing was used to express spiritual ideas. Like Prometheus, who brought fire from Heaven, Odin spied the runes. The runes would change as they drifted across vast distances to be met ashore in strange lands and greeted by inquisitive and open minds who would adapt, integrate, use, and change them. Confronting and integrating the unknown requires a certain amount of bravery. Even as witches are brave by nature, engaging with ideas and rituals on the fringe of mainstream society, always captivating with their allure, always being called back into existence and popularity, they are still feared. Magick swims through the astral plane, planting itself firmly on the earth the minute it finds a conduit, such as a mystical language with a skilled and dedicated practitioner, by which to break through.

Flip through this book and choose a rune system with a phonetic element. Start with the letters of your magickal name, the one that best describes your true nature. Pronounce it softly, like in a whisper. If you are unsure of how something is supposed to sound, just hiss. Get in touch with the primal parts of your brain as well as the frontal cortex. Feel the electricity sparkling through the neural network of your brain. Hiss and awaken the sacred serpent of forbidden knowledge. Go for it. Feel kundalini energy rising through your body as you breathe life into time itself. Say your name.

As you memorize the sound of your name, picture the linear form of each rune. You have been practicing visualization, so you should be adept at this. As you pronounce, imagine each one igniting in a line of hot blue fire, sparkling with energy. You experience your name not only through sound but also through sight. You envision fire because you know it is hot, and you allow yourself to envision and feel this heat, engaging another level of sensory perception. You are seeing. You are listening. You are feeling. You are knowing. Now you are ready to reach beyond.

The sound you are hearing? What does it look like? How do the patterns interlock to form meaning? You are now ready to create. With all that you have allowed yourself to see, now you must look beyond. What is the sound of the thing you cannot see? Let a new vision come into your mind, one from the unseen realm. Now write it down. This will be the beginning of a new form, one that you have created out of nurturing your psychic vision.

### Finding Your Aesthetic

You can determine your own aesthetic for creating an original runic alphabet. Some simple tools you will want to use are a straightedge or ruler, a French curve, a compass, or all of the above. Think of the beauty of different font styles, and choose features that appeal to you. Look at sheet music for another example of symbols that represent sounds inscribed on a series of staves. Pick a general motif for consistency, either linear or round, and see how many variations you can come up with. Think about the relationships between symbols and their frequency of use. You may want to depart from traditional alphabetic order and instead develop your symbols according to frequency of use. Try starting with the five vowel sounds and see what your mind and heart wish to produce.

Another source of inspiration you will want to explore is the palm of your own hand. Examine your palm and look for patterns of crossed lines, intersecting lines, lines that touch, and lines that curve. As you discover repeating patterns, look closely for subtle variations. You may find that the beginning of your own rune system has already been written and that you are already in possession of it. Think of the relation of lines to each other and where on your hand they occur. A simple online perusal of palmistry will tell you which lines relate to love, family, choices, and your path.

### Druid Hand Signals

The scholar and poet Robert Graves suggested that Druids could communicate using hand signals for the Ogham runes, as he noted that the number and relationships inherent in the system corresponded neatly with the different segments of the fingers. He suggested that communication could be made silently by spelling words just by pointing to the place on the hand where a particular rune would be represented. It is interesting to note that in his theory of runic sign language, he suggested that the symbols appeared in reverse order. Instead of moving from right to left, as is widely accepted, Graves suggests that Druids may have indicated runes by touching the hand from left to right.

Think about what makes the most sense to you. Western alphabetic systems tend to move from left to right, while many Eastern languages, ancient and modern, move from right to left. Choose the orientation that is natural to you so that you are not having to relearn relationship in addition to the task of creation and assigning meaning.

When you have settled on an aesthetic and general form, you can start to draft your original runes in earnest. Use your grimoire and, with the straightedge, create a neat table, and begin to populate it with information. For example, create a table with three columns. The left column will contain your symbols. The center column will contain their associated pronunciation or alphabetic equivalent. Finally, in the third column, you will record their meaning.

# ASSIGNING SYMBOLS TO EACH RUNE

As your ability to visualize is perfected, the next step is to manifest. Manifesting is the act of bringing or channeling ideas from the unseen realm and ushering them in to perceivable reality. Think of a drawing or a poem. It begins as an idea that takes form. As it takes on its unseen form, it begins to develop specific characteristics. As these charactcristics crystallize, they are able to be described. Once they are able to be described, they are able to be inscribed.

By inscribing the unseen, you make the inspiration perceivable to others.

This is a rewarding and immensely validating experience. There is a particular unrivaled pleasure in creation. It is as central to life as any offering to the greater good. Think of the desire to mate. Life demands more of itself, and when the life force is flowing strongly, communing with it can bring states of profound pleasure and the fruits of generative activities.

This process is not limited to sexual or biological activities. Communion with spirit and oracles and interacting in a metaphysical realm can be intensely pleasurable and creatively fulfilling. Comparing it to earthly pleasures makes it easier to understand and gives practitioners an entry point. Spiritual witches will be familiar with the Charge of the Goddess, which states that all acts of love and pleasure are considered acts of worship and are evidence of dedication to the path. This is a sharp departure from most other belief systems that emphasize deprivation, abstinence, and asceticism. It can be unsettling to accept pleasurable acts as sacred when so many people get the idea ingrained into their minds that pleasure and its accompanying creations are somehow immoral, imprudent, or wrong.

Accepting yourself as a creative being whose contributions to the body of occult knowledge and wisdom are valid and needed opens up a whole new range of possibilities for magickal expression. Today, many of us have concerns about the implications of cultural appropriation, even as we acknowledge the very human and very historically consistent tendency for people to adapt other cultures and practices to their own (one need not look any further than Classical Greek and Roman mythology or Babylonian and Sumerian patterns of worship, where many deities are practically interchangeable). Accepting the ability of the individual to create is one way to avoid this issue altogether. Think about every divination system used today. Tarot cards were drawn and interpreted by people. Planchettes and spirit boards are made by people. Pendulums are made by people. Scripture was written by people. It is widely accepted that all of these very different avenues all lead to a world beyond our imagining, infused with spirit. There is nothing that prohibits a magick practitioner from developing and using their own system of runes. Runes are one of the most enduring methods of divination, and they deserve to be reinterpreted and reinvented for the modern age, and there is no one better to take on that level of sacred work than the people who love the runes and know them well.

---

### Rune Casters and Rune-Masters

As you continue to grow in your practice of using runes for divination, you may find yourself able to create and interpret new kinds of spreads. Learning runes is similar to learning a new language. You will enter into a relationship with them. They will speak to you and you will speak through them. Once you have this new language and psychic skill well developed, you may wish to teach others. Being able to cast and interpret a rune spread is one type of skill. Being able to teach this skill to others is another type of ability.

---

## Creating Runes

Creating your own runes and assigning symbols bears a similarity to creating sigils, which is a widely accepted practice of witchcraft on both the secular and spiritual levels. Think of the relative simplicity of the characters of the Ogham runes. Your designs do not need to be complex in order to be useful and effective. In fact, there is a particular beauty to simplicity, as it lends an ease of memorization to the process. You can begin alphabetically, mirroring the sound and sequence of your mother tongue, or you can determine your starting point by frequency of use, beginning with the most frequently used sounds and symbols.

If you want to create a twenty-four-symbol system, think of it as six groups of four characters. Each group of four can share a common motif or characteristic, such as two sets of characters with intersecting lines, two sets with diagonal lines, or two sets with curved lines. Look to the aicme of the Ogham runes for inspiration and notice how each family is an inversion or expansion of another. Think about the different activities presented in this book and consider which ones you may want to adapt.

If you want to create a physical set of runes on wood tiles, then you can use any variation of shape that you can draw. If you want to try the metal runes, linear characters will be the easiest to transpose to this medium using the methods described in Chapter 12.

## USING YOUR OWN RUNES FOR DIVINATION

Just as you did in previous chapters, you now have to take the time to envision what your symbols represent. If you are visually oriented, the challenge can be articulating your associative meaning. Use the Witch runes for inspiration. As you have already learned, the symbols do not need to be complex; they just need to make sense to you. You may first consider what the image represents, such as a half-moon shape representing a cup, then you can ascribe a dedicated meaning, such as "the heart" or "love." When you draw this particular rune (or your own original equivalent), you know that you are dealing with matters of the heart. Think of how the Ogham runes are organized into families much like the tarot is organized in suits. Creating a system that adheres to rules will make it easier to use.

Divination is just another form of communication, except that you cannot visually see the entity with which you are speaking. Think of the symbols and patterns that are already familiar to you and let them be your guide. Complex does not necessarily mean better and there is a reassuring beauty in simplicity.

As you continue to explore, create, define, and express yourself through runes, you may discover more ways to use them than are described here. Once you have learned these systems and have fully integrated them into your consciousness so that you are able to teach others your methods, you are on your way to becoming a rune-master. Blessed be your path, and may the timeless wisdom of the runes forever be your guide.

# REFERENCES

Agrippa, Heinrich Cornelius. *Declamation on the Nobility and Preeminence of the Female Sex.* Edited and translated by Albert Rabil Jr. Chicago: University of Chicago Press, 1996.

Blum, Ralph. *The Book of Runes.* New York: St. Martin's Press, 1983.

Čuk, Jaka. "Archaeological Evidence for the Beginning of the Norse Colony in Greenland." Master's thesis, University of Iceland, 2020. http://hdl.handle.net/1946/34937.

Daniels, Peter T., and William Bright, eds. *The World's Writing Systems.* New York: Oxford University Press, 1996.

Findell, Martin. *Runes.* London: The British Museum Press, 2014.

Foster, Justin. "Huld Manuscript of Galdrastafir Witchcraft Magic Symbols and Runes - English Translation." Academia.edu. June 15, 2015. Accessed Sept 14, 2021. www.academia.edu/13008560/Huld Manuscript_of_Galdrastafir_Witchcraft_Magic_Symbols_and_Runes_-_English_Translation.

Granholm, Kennet. "The Rune-Gild: Heathenism, Traditionalism, and the Left-Hand Path." *International Journal for the Study of New Religions* 1, no. 10 (July 29, 2010): 95–115. https://doi.org/10.1558/ijsnr.v1i1.95.

Graves, Charles, and C. Limerick. "The Ogham Alphabet." *Hermathena* 2, no. 4 (1876): pp. 443–72. www.jstor.org/stable/23036451.

Graves, Robert. *The White Goddess: A Historical Grammar of Poetic Myth.* New York: Farrar, Straus and Giroux, 1948.

McKinnell, John, Klaus Düwel, and Rudolf Simek. *Runes, Magic and Religion: A Sourcebook.* Studia Medievalia Septentrionalia. Vienna: Fassbender, 2004.

Näsström, Britt-Mari. "Magical Music in Old Norse Literature." *Scripta Instituti Donneriani Aboensis* 16 (January 1, 1996): 229–40. https://doi.org/10.30674/scripta.67231.

Norse Mythology for Smart People. "The Meanings of the Runes." Accessed June 28, 2021. http://norse-mythology.org/runes/ The-Meanings-of-the-Runes/.

Page, R.I. *An Introduction to English Runes.* 2nd ed. Suffolk, UK: Boydell & Brewer, Limited, 1999. Reprinted in paperback 2006.

Page, R.I. "The Old English Rune *Eoh, Íh, 'Yew-Tree.'" Medium Ævum* 37, no. 2 (1968): 125–36. https://doi.org/10.2307/43627424.

Vebæk, Christian L. *Narsaq: A Norse Landnáma Farm.* Greenland: The Commission for Scientific Research in Greenland, 1993.

# US/METRIC
# CONVERSION CHARTS

## LENGTH CONVERSIONS

| US Length Measure | Metric Equivalent |
| --- | --- |
| ¼ inch | 0.6 centimeters |
| ½ inch | 1.2 centimeters |
| ¾ inch | 1.9 centimeters |
| 1 inch | 2.5 centimeters |
| 1 ½ inches | 3.8 centimeters |
| 1 foot | 0.3 meters |
| 1 yard | 0.9 meters |

## WEIGHT CONVERSIONS

| US Weight Measure | Metric Equivalent |
| --- | --- |
| ½ ounce | 15 grams |
| 1 ounce | 30 grams |
| 2 ounces | 60 grams |
| 3 ounces | 85 grams |
| ¼ pound (4 ounces) | 115 grams |
| ½ pound (8 ounces) | 225 grams |
| ¾ pound (12 ounces) | 340 grams |
| 1 pound (16 ounces) | 454 grams |

| BAKING PAN SIZES | |
|---|---|
| **US** | **Metric** |
| 8 x 1 1/2 inch round baking pan | 20 x 4 cm cake tin |
| 9 x 1 1/2 inch round baking pan | 23 x 3.5 cm cake tin |
| 11 x 7 x 1 1/2 inch baking pan | 28 x 18 x 4 cm baking tin |
| 13 x 9 x 2 inch baking pan | 30 x 20 x 5 cm baking tin |
| 2 quart rectangular baking dish | 30 x 20 x 3 cm baking tin |
| 15 x 10 x 2 inch baking pan | 30 x 25 x 2 cm baking tin (Swiss roll tin) |
| 9 inch pie plate | 22 x 4 or 23 x 4 cm pie plate |
| 7 or 8 inch springform pan | 18 or 20 cm springform or loose bottom cake tin |
| 9 x 5 x 3 inch loaf pan | 23 x 13 x 7 cm or 2 lb narrow loaf or pate tin |
| 1 1/2 quart casserole | 1.5 liter casserole |
| 2 quart casserole | 2 liter casserole |

| OVEN TEMPERATURE CONVERSIONS | |
|---|---|
| **Degrees Fahrenheit** | **Degrees Celsius** |
| 200 degrees F | 95 degrees C |
| 250 degrees F | 120 degrees C |
| 275 degrees F | 135 degrees C |
| 300 degrees F | 150 degrees C |
| 325 degrees F | 160 degrees C |
| 350 degrees F | 180 degrees C |
| 375 degrees F | 190 degrees C |
| 400 degrees F | 205 degrees C |
| 425 degrees F | 220 degrees C |
| 450 degrees F | 230 degrees C |

| VOLUME CONVERSIONS | |
|---|---|
| **US Volume Measure** | **Metric Equivalent** |
| ⅛ teaspoon | 0.5 milliliter |
| ¼ teaspoon | 1 milliliter |
| ½ teaspoon | 2 milliliters |
| 1 teaspoon | 5 milliliters |
| ½ tablespoon | 7 milliliters |
| 1 tablespoon (3 teaspoons) | 15 milliliters |
| 2 tablespoons (1 fluid ounce) | 30 milliliters |
| ¼ cup (4 tablespoons) | 60 milliliters |
| ⅓ cup | 90 milliliters |
| ½ cup (4 fluid ounces) | 125 milliliters |
| ⅔ cup | 160 milliliters |
| ¾ cup (6 fluid ounces) | 180 milliliters |
| 1 cup (16 tablespoons) | 250 milliliters |
| 1 pint (2 cups) | 500 milliliters |
| 1 quart (4 cups) | 1 liter (about) |

# INDEX

# About the Author

Judy Ann Nock is the author of six books on witchcraft. She holds a master of science degree in TESOL from the City College of New York and has a double bachelor's degree in creative writing and theatre from Florida State University. Her numerous works have been referenced in *The New York Times*, *Publishers Weekly*, *The Guardian*, Yahoo.com, *Bust*, *Luna Luna*, *HelloGiggles*, and *Bustle*, among others, and she has appeared in feature articles in *Refinery29* and *The Village Voice*. She also performs regularly with the critically acclaimed Hoboken cave punk supergroup known as Psych-O-Positive. Radio stations such as WFMU, WFDU, WBAI, and Strong Island Radio have dedicated airplay to her music, books, and life experiences. Nock is also an accomplished metalsmith and diamond expert with a diploma from the Gemological Institute of America, as well as a member of American Mensa. She lives with her daughter in New York City.

# POWERFUL HERBS FOR THE
# MODERN-DAY WITCH!

# PICK UP OR DOWNLOAD YOUR COPY TODAY!